RECONSTRUCTION IN PSYCHOANALYSIS

RECONSTRUCTION IN PSYCHOANALYSIS

Childhood Revisited and Recreated

Harold P. Blum, M.D.

International Universities Press, Inc.
Madison   Connecticut

International Universities Press and IUP (&design)® are registered trademarks of International Universities Press, Inc.

Library of Congress Cataloging-in-Publication Data

Blum, Harold P., 1929-
    Reconstruction in psychoanalysis: childhood revisited and recreated/Harold P. Blum.
      p. cm.
    Includes bibliographical references and index.
    ISBN 0-8236-5783-3
    1. Reconstruction (Psychoanalysis) I. Title.
RC489.R39B58 1994
616.89'17—dc20   93-38933
                                         CIP

Manufactured in the United States of America

Contents

Preface

This monograph was proposed by a research group on reconstruction, under the auspices of the Psychoanalytic Research and Development Fund, and draws on its deliberations and discussions. The research was conducted over a period of five years from 1980 to 1985. The members were invited to participate based upon their scholarship, expertise, and interest in the psychoanalytic research, and their anticipated contribution to it. The group met monthly during the academic year under my chairmanship. Following my own writings and interests, I had also suggested the topic and initial research issues. As we pursued an organized, systematic investigation of the theory, technique, and concept of reconstruction in an independent setting, the atmosphere was that of an open forum, with clinical analytic data, and extemporaneous commentary and review. The other members of the group were: Drs. Samuel Abrams, Martin Bergmann, Donald Cohen, Alvin Frank, Sidney Furst, Marjorie Harley, Selma Kramer, Marianne Kris, John McDevitt, Peter Neubauer, Henry Nunberg, Mortimer Ostow, Bernard Pacella, Leonard Shengold, Arthur Valenstein, and Annemarie Weil. The group inquiry was a continuing source of inspiration, information, and analytic education, so valuable to the construction of this monograph. In thanking the entire group for their stimulating and enriching individual and collective contributions, I am mindful of the necessarily personal, univocal character of my exposition. This work necessarily conveys my own considerations, ideas, formulations, and synthesis, for which I accept full responsibility. The volume cannot reconstruct the group process, nor can it fully represent the individual members' views, or the collective analytic research.

Drs. Alvin Frank and Annemarie Weil provided very sagacious comments and suggestions, for which I am deeply appreciative. The aim of the research was further to understand and clarify reconstruction and seek its application and integration with other clinical, technical, and theoretical perspectives. The principles of reconstruction and its mode of therapeutic action were to be elucidated. The subject was intriguing because reconstruction was so important to an understanding of personality development and disorder, yet it seemed to be in relative eclipse in psychoanalytic practice and education. The term was scarcely cited or used in clinical reports, clinical discourse, and psychoanalytic supervision. Reconstruction had been little discussed in the recent psychoanalytic literature and had received scant attention in contemporary texts on psychoanalytic technique.

The renewed interest in reconstruction corrects this imbalance, again focuses attention on the importance of childhood and the analysis of the infantile roots of unconscious conflict. New attention to the developmental point of view and the controversies surounding pathogenesis and different analytic theories have all supported the value and utilization of reconstruction. The exponentially increasing knowledge of infant development and advancing developmental research with contributions from many different disciplines have led to extraordinary efforts to utilize and integrate these new findings into analytic theory and to apply the new findings to the process of reconstruction. The developmental research has also converged with interest in preoedipal psychopathology and preoedipal contributions to later personality disturbance, with efforts at more refined preoedipal reconstruction.

Reconstruction has also been related to a number of current theoretical controversies. Often stated as historical truth versus narrative truth or fact versus fantasy, the controversies involve psychic versus external reality, subjectivity and objectivity, and causality versus meaning—the validity and theoretical position assigned to reconstruction is closely related to the controversy concerning natural science versus hermeneutic models of psychoanalysis. Controversy concerning reconstruction is also related to the overriding transference significance of the "here and now" versus the childish nature of transference and the vast importance of childhood for the understanding of personality development and disorder.

The appreciation of different interpretations of events and meanings, and accretions and transformations of meaning in different phases of development, and different phases of life, and indeed in different phases of analysis, has converged within an expanded current appreciation of analysis as a two-person process. The analyst's predilections, his interest in reconstruction, his preferences or bias in observation and formulation, and the analyst's values will all influence reconstruction. As in interpretation, countertransference has a significant role in reconstruction, especially if intrusive conflicts and a hidden analytic agenda remain outside of awareness. However, there is no last word, and reconstructions are always subject to remodeling. Reconstruction remains an essential and fruitful part of analytic work. Allied to both developmental considerations and genetic interpretation, reconstruction bridges past and present, causality and meaning, fantasy and actual experience. Without recon-struction, interpretation would lack historical context and comprehension of the changing but persisting influence of unconscious conflict and trauma throughout the life cycle. Just as there is no complete analysis, there is no complete and ultimate reconstruction. The quality and precision of reconstruction has changed with advances in psychoanalysis, and, for example, the reconstructions in Freud's classic case histories continue to be amplified and modified in successive analytic studies.

Chapter One

Introduction to Reconstruction in Psychoanalysis

In recent years, after long neglect, there has been some revival of interest in reconstruction. An interest in history, in roots, in pathogenesis, and in developmental pathways and outcomes is related to reconstruction. Throughout the history of psychoanalysis, analysts and patients have pondered the question of where the patient was coming from, and how he or she got there. Attempts at reconstruction are universal because curiosity is universal, not only curiosity about the child's origins, but also about parental origins, and personal and familial history. Just as there are legends about the origins of nations and peoples, so too are there individual, personal myths (Kris, 1956b), and familial myths which are, in effect, fantasy reconstructions. These reconstructions are also related to the search for causality and continuity and represent an attempt to explain how the present developed from the influences of the past. From its inception, reconstruction was therefore linked to the discovery of the significance of childhood for all subsequent development. The genetic and the developmental points of view were intrinsic to the concept and process of reconstruction. With newer structural and developmental thinking, analytic experience with patients during different periods of life and different forms of disturbance, e.g., borderline, and the exponential expansion of infant and child psychiatric research, increased attention is now being paid to the relationship of developmental knowledge to reconstruction and the impact of reconstruction upon advances in psychoanalytic developmental theory. Regression does not simply reproduce earlier states unaltered, and analytic theory and practice have long been complemented by observational research. The reconstruction of infantile life takes into account the stages of cognitive development leading toward abstract thinking; affect development leading from simple to complex affects; the emergence of signal anxiety; the emergence of self criticism, guilt, and remorse; the evolution of identity; the use of I and me; and the use of language structure with subject, object, verb, and inferences concerning intrapsychic self and object representations.

Developmental theory has also been closely linked to clinical interest in oedipal issues and the preoedipal antecedents of the Oedipus complex; but it has also been linked with later developmental phases. Contemporary studies of borderline conditions and pathological narcissism have converged with studies of preoedipal problems. These studies in turn have led to clinical inferences of primordial transference, to reconstructions concerning earliest development, and to problems of reorganization and developmental transformation. Object relations theory, the concept of separation-individuation, and the challenges of self psychology all stimulated and activated a focus on genetic reconstruction. Thus, reconstruction was related to several analytic theories, and, within traditional analysis, to contrasting emphasis upon the here-and-now and fantasy elaboration. The lectures, publications, and teaching of members of the research group may also have contributed to the revival of interest in reconstruction. The group was interested in these issues but also the more general questions concerning reconstruction in the context of contemporary psychoanalysis as well as in a historical perspective.

Among the questions asked were these:

1. Why has there been renewed interest recently in reconstruction, after a long period of relative neglect?
2. How should reconstruction be defined? What are the conceptual boundaries of reconstruction?
3. What is the difference between reconstruction and interpretation, particularly genetic interpretation?
4. How has the concept of reconstruction changed with the development of psychoanalytic theory and technique?
5. Has there been a reciprocal influence between reconstruction and psychoanalytic developmental theory?
6. Why is reconstruction clinically necessary and often compelling? What is the use (and possible abuse) of reconstruction in analytic work?
7. Is reconstruction required for all patients, or is reconstruction of greater significance in those patients who have been traumatized or have experienced pathogenic object relations and deviant development?
8. How do we reconstruct? What is the difference between construction and reconstruction?
9. When do we reconstruct? Can reconstruction be useful in the opening phase as it was in the pioneer era of psychoanalysis?
10. What is the therapeutic mode and strategy of reconstruction? How are the therapeutic effects of reconstruction achieved?
11. What is the significance of the reconstruction of external reality for the clarification of psychic reality? How does reconstruction contribute to the understanding and coordination of the patient's external and internal worlds?

12. How important is reconstruction of the patient's current life situation, for example, of the adult precipitation or exacerbation of the patient's neurosis?
13. Are there particular forms of analytic data (e.g., dreams, transference phenomena, screen memories) that facilitate reconstruction, or does reconstruction rest on the totality of the analytic process?
14. How is reconstruction validated? How significant is an accompanying sense of conviction?
15. What is the role of reconstruction in child and adolescent analysis?
16. How important is reconstruction of adolescence in adult analysis?
17. How accurate, reliable, and effective are preoedipal reconstructions? Are reconstructions of the preverbal period possible and analytically useful?
18. What is the relationship of reconstruction to theories of pathogenesis?

The relationship of reconstruction to the genetic–developmental points of view proved to be intrinsically connected with attempts to explore and explain the infantile roots of later personality disturbance. Patients and analysts often knew intuitively that endowment influenced experience in a selective fashion and that "something happened" or that there were significant "happenings" and formative experiences. But it was a most difficult task to know when and what had occurred and to identify developmental landmarks and both causal and chronological sequences. The actual facts might never be ascertained. Reconstruction deals with the creation as well as the recreation of the past, one which is altered in the process of reconstruction. The past is not discovered, retrieved, or recaptured in its pristine form. The analyst is, of course, concerned with latent psychological meaning, dynamic issues, and developmental consequences, so that factual history tends to recede into the raw material of reconstruction. To the external observer, the birth of twin siblings when the patient was 2 years old may be a simple historical fact, but may have had enormous psychological impact upon the patient and his or her parents. A family movie taken at the time of the twins' birth would reveal little—at best no more than the outer surface of the patient's complex inner reactions, which would be the object of later analytic reconstruction.

The terms *reconstruction* and *construction* were used synonymously by Freud (1918, 1937), and both terms had multiple meanings. The analyst formulated constructions in his own mind, and this was a silent part of the analytic work; the analyst transmitted reconstructions to the patient as an explicit technical intervention; patient and analyst shared efforts, frequently indirectly and piecemeal, in the process and refinement of reconstruction. In addition, the analyst might use reconstruction to propose, confirm, or challenge a theoretical or developmental hypothesis. The Isakower (1938) phenomenon is an example of a reconstruction that was subsequently reviewed and utilized in related analytic research. Freud (1937) referred succinctly to all these meanings of reconstruction:

> [The analyst's] task is to make out what has been forgotten from the traces which it has left behind or, more correctly, to *construct* it. The time and manner in which he conveys his constructions to the person who is being analysed, as well as the explanations with which he accompanies them, constitute the link between the two portions of the work of analysis, between his own part and that of the patient.
>
> His work of construction, or, if it is preferred, of reconstruction, resembles to a great extent an archaeologist's excavation of some dwelling-place that has been destroyed and buried or of some ancient edifice [pp. 258–259].

Freud often used an archaeological model of psychoanalytic reconstruction and suggested that analytic reconstruction was in some respects easier. The analyst "works under more favourable conditions than the archaeologist" and can depend upon "repetitions of reactions dating from infancy" which appear inside and outside the analysis (1937, p. 259). The living patient could contribute to and correct reconstruction. Considering that nothing in mental life can perish and that everything is preserved and can be brought to light, Freud (1930) cautiously reflected: "The fact remains that only in the mind is such a preservation of all the earlier stages alongside the final form possible. . . . Perhaps we are going too far in this. Perhaps we ought to content ourselves with asserting that what is past in mental life *may* be preserved and is not *necessarily* destroyed" (p. 71). These issues would stimulate later research relevant to reconstruction. The remodeling of structure and representations that were still subject to developmental change also highlighted differences between archaeological models and the process of reconstruction. Modern archaeology, like psychoanalysis, is far more concerned with dynamic and developmental inferences concerning society and culture, for example, with life-styles and art styles, than with the static forms of relics and the dates of historical events.

Psychoanalysis has implicitly used other models of reconstruction, and I would particularly propose the evidence, inferences, and theory of evolution. Darwinian theory rested on a reconstruction of successively earlier genetically ordered phases and a developmental progression inferred from early observational evidence. The evidential clues, for example, in fossils, might be quite rare and remote and rest on minute details or persisting traces. Regressive features might reappear as atavisms, and earlier forms might overlap with new features and organization. Even before precise chemical DNA analysis was possible, evolutionary biology had utilized a meticulous, cohesive process of reconstruction, suggestive of psychoanalytic reconstruction. Analytic and evolutionary thought converged in genetic reconstruction and developmental propositions. No one piece of evidence or bit of data might be sufficient for the theory of evolution, but the mass of evidence and the sequential ordering and organization of data led to both scientific conviction and practical application.

While, as I mentioned earlier, Freud (1937, p. 259) used the terms *reconstruction* and *construction* synonymously, Greenacre (1975) preferred to retain the term *construction* for the analyst's initial, tentative formulations concerning neurosogenesis and the patient's history. Constructions were preliminary, private analytic hypotheses. Constructions were the foundation for reconstruction and became reconstructions when the analyst intervened by presenting the reconstruction to the patient in the analytic process. Patients also reciprocally offered their own reconstructions and would sometimes attempt to expand or validate reconstruction with extra-analytic source material such as parents' recollections or diaries. The reconstruction was to extend the domain of analytic understanding of the patient's inner life and actual history. It aimed to regain and restore the inarticulate, lost experience consistent with factual history. An inferred historic truth was obtained, bearing in mind that it was inexact and prey to subjective interpretation. Though the methodology was radically altered, the use of reconstruction in applications of psychoanalytic thought outside the analytic situation, in archaeology, art, and literature, became commonplace.

Reconstruction was historically embedded in a theory of therapy based upon the catharsis of repressed trauma. Seduction traumas were thought to cause later neurotic disturbance, and the traumatic experience, the associated strangulated affects, and the causal connections

7

between past and present, were outside the patient's awareness. The buried traumatic experience was to be lifted from repression and then could be remembered or reconstructed from the traces left behind. When it was realized that the supposed sexual trauma was not always fact but sometimes fantasy or a mixture of the two, an exclusive traumatic theory of pathogenesis was relinquished. As a consequence, reconstruction, at least of core traumatic episodes, could be as suspect as the putative, ubiquitous reports and reconstructions of seduction.

Actually, after Freud's agonizing reappraisal of this preanalytic theory and therapy, a correction and refinement of reconstruction contributed to the elaboration of drive theory. Attention shifted away from environmental influence to psychosexual development and its culmination in the Oedipus complex. A balance had to be restored between exclusively intrapsychic and environmentalist points of view, taking into account both psychic reality and the inevitable fantasy distortion and elaboration of actual experience. If used naively, and inappropriately, reconstruction could impede rather than promote the psychoanalytic process.

It may be noted that the issues of fantasy versus reality, fact versus fiction, and historical truth or narrative truth would resurface in new form. Reconstruction straddled the inner and outer worlds, both psychic reality and material reality (Freud, 1916–1917). Although traumatic experiences were no longer the object of exclusive reconstructive focus, it was apparent that reconstruction was still essential to psychoanalytic work. However, the model of reconstruction which Freud had so innovatively and successfully employed in his own self-analysis and initial analytic work with patients, changed with advances in theory and technique. Even in his last and major paper on the subject, Freud's (1937) return to an archaeological model, and his emphasis on persisting traces rather than developmental transformations, left the process of reconstruction straddling the past and future of psychoanalysis.

As attention centered upon the inner life and the universal and personal fantasies of childhood, it became necessary to understand the form, content, and historical context of unconscious fantasy and its conscious derivatives. The universal experience of sex differences and sibling birth had characteristic and idiosyncratic representation in unconscious fantasy. This raised new questions about the role of reconstruction in relation to the universal and the unique in development; to special sensitivities, tendencies, and predispositions; and to the relation between endowment and experience, the influence of trauma and special impressions, developmental phase, phase specificity, and phase organization and disorganizaton. The changing meaning of traumas over time, and the reshaping of significant experience in fantasies of later development, had begun to be considered by Freud; for example, in the evolution of adult beating fantasy (1919). The role of developmental transformations and structural change, not entirely dependent upon previous antecedents, proved to be central to ongoing discussions. Unconscious fantasy was subject to developmental vicissitudes, and replaced discrete memory in transference analysis and reconstruction. There was no straight line or linear sequence in reconstruction from present to past. There was even greater complexity from the developmental perspective, in which the transformations from infancy to adult life were considered, with interacting alterations and possible discontinuities.

Many interesting issues concerning reconstruction applied to discrete events. Could a discrete event such as an infantile illness or sexual abuse actually be reconstructed with approximate historical detail, as well as its unconscious fantasy meaning and impact upon subsequent development? Would not such a reconstruction have important analytic and therapeutic significance? Kris (1956c) had stressed the importance of patterning and the absorption and alteration of specific events in the course of development. In contrast to Greenacre (1956), he doubted that the "seduction on the staircase" could be accurately reconstructed in later life from the data of adult psychoanalysis. Disturbance could be phase-related but subject to regressive alteration and pathogenic reinforcement or to beneficial reorganization in later phases. Reconstruction could therefore amplify and contribute to the understanding of the origins of the patient's disturbance, provided that the reconstruction resolved rather than intensified resistance. The reconstruction had to emerge from and articulate with the analytic data, reciprocally expanding the explanatory power and reach of the analysis.

In its typical form, reconstruction is a genetic proposition which supplies new information to the patient about his past in a way which furthers the psychoanalytic process and self-knowledge. An immediate question then is the difference between reconstruction and interpretation in general, but particularly between reconstruction and genetic interpretation. To what degree do reconstruction and genetic interpretation differ and to what degree do they overlap? Another major question refers to the difference between reconstruction and remembering, between an analytic proposition and the patient's actual memory. The issues that relate to a differentiation between reconstruction and interpretation and between reconstruction and memory, largely derive from Freud's (1937) paper on the subject, "Constructions in Analysis."

A genetic interpretation may deal with a repressed, infantile impulse such as a desire to bite and devour the analyst. The patient may or may not have memories related to infantile biting and oral incorporation, but the fantasy can be recovered, and its infantile nature will become apparent. Reconstruction, however, applies to those genetic interventions where the patient does not specifically recapture and recall infantile fantasy and experience. Using all the data of the analysis such as transference, dreams, screen memories, and fragments of memory, the analyst synthesizes the analytic evidence to reconstruct a piece of the patient's past. As an integrated act, a reconstruction is therefore far more complicated than a genetic interpretation; reconstruction may amalgamate a number of clarifications achieved in several genetic interpretations. Reconstruction is thus a form of genetic intervention that replaces memory and which expands and reciprocally orders genetic interpretation. According to Freud (1937), reconstruction may have all the power of conviction associated with overcoming infantile amnesia and directly remembering the past.

Reconstruction establishes causal connections between past and present, integrating fantasy and reality and coordinating actual experience with its unconscious meaning and intrapsychic fantasy interpretation. Reconstruction has an explanatory value for the patient and for the analyst, and can clarify the meaning of core conflict, fantasies, and actual experience. The process of reconstruction leads to greater clarification, coherence, and both historical and psychological continuity. With less emphasis upon the recovery of childhood memories, the integrative analytic work of reconstruction assumes ever greater significance in the unfolding of the analytic process. In fact, a question which has repeatedly arisen concerns reconstruction both as a specific, technical intervention and as an overarching explanatory framework which tends to merge with the analytic process itself.

Reconstruction provides a base from which the analyst infers the infantile neurotic conflicts and traumas as they are recapitulated in transference, dreams, symptoms, and in the patient's character and neurotic behavior inside and outside the analysis. The historical basis of transference and resistance is determined in the process of reconstruction, so that reconstruction offers some guidance for the locus of analytic work. As a genetic explanation, reconstruction depends upon the correlation and coordination of analytic data, with clarification of the history proceeding with the testing of the reconstruction in the analytic process. In the subsequent analytic work, reconstruction becomes a joint composition of analyst and patient. A cohesive statement can be formulated that orchestrates and organizes disparate data bearing on the patient's life and problems; for example, a meaningful linking of the patient's fear of success, passive inhibition, avoidance of competition, castration anxiety, and oral-dependent regression. The analytic work increasingly demands this particular reconstruction from among the alternatives, with a more exacting and illuminating fit with the revised, expanded analytic autobiography. Since there is no simple connection, "no straight line," between past and present disturbance, and reconstruction draws on multiple perspectives, it follows that a reconstruction will be longer than an interpretation, and of a higher order of complexity and integration.

How discrete does a reconstruction have to be in order to be so categorized and to fit the definition? Parallel to inexact interpretation, how much conviction could analyst and patient really have about discrete reconstructions of the events, fantasies, and inner experiences of remote periods of life unsupported by definite memories? These questions were also balanced and complicated by questions about the process of memory itself, its registration, encoding, and retrieval. Memory itself was subject to screening and distortion, and Freud (1899) had pondered whether all memory should not be designated as being in part fantasy since memory and fantasy were, in degree, created in the present act of remembrance. Memory was not necessarily recalled accurately, completely, or in a meaningful context and affective relationship. Fragmentation and isolation of memories occurred, along with an opposite telescoping or condensation of many experiences into one memory. Since memory was not reliable, and did not always carry a sense of conviction for the patient, neither were the memories of family and friends any more reliable. Some of the same questions about memory reappeared in relation to reconstruction, though a reconstructive process had been implicit in analytic work on both the repressed and the remembered past. The analysis and synthesis of memory actually involved reconstruction.

The question of whether reconstruction really had the same status and the same conviction in analytic work as transference recapitulation gained in importance. Memory recall as a goal of analysis was to give way to the primacy of analysis of unconscious conflict, particularly in the form of transference conflict. Excessive or exclusive focus on transference could diminish attention to reconstruction and other significant extra-transference issues. Problems of conviction, whether of reconstruction, memory, or transference meaning, reappeared in different forms throughout the research group deliberations. Although there was concern about creating or superimposing an analytic myth about the hypothetical past, there was a converging consensus about the importance of reconstruction for the understanding of both the analyst and the patient, and its facilitating effect on the analytic process.

Since free association in the analytic process inevitably led to childhood and to the analytic task of reconstructing the forgotten fantasies and experiences of childhood from the traces left behind (Freud, 1937), could there be a psychoanalytic process without reconstruction?

Was clinical psychoanalysis conceivable without reconstruction? Could the psychoanalytic process have been discovered without reconstruction? A number of parallel questions were of direct relevance. Why do we reconstruct, and why are we compelled to do so in the course of analytic work? How and when do we reconstruct? Do we reconstruct with all patients or only with some analysands who have certain types of psychopathology or analysands with particular gifts for autobiography and historical synthesis? As these questions were pondered, the tendency to equate reconstruction with the analytic process itself appeared anew. The goal of analysis might be one grand reconstruction, although the reductionism and oversimplification of such an idealized reconstruction were usually readily apparent. Since reconstruction might at various points in the analysis guide and influence the analyst's interpretations, reconstruction could facilitate interpretation. In the sense of a developmental model of the infantile neurosis, reconstruction might at times be superordinate to interpretation. Reconstructed models of the patient's childhood, however, should not preempt but enrich other dimensions of analytic thought and work.

The tendency to fuse and confuse the process of reconstruction with the analytic process proved to be counterbalanced by the opposite and more general tendency to focus almost exclusively on the transference in contemporary analysis. Indeed, for many analysts, the transference threatened to become the "be all and end all" of analytic work. If there was a "royal road" to the analysis of unconscious conflict, it was via the transference. In this frame of reference, transference analysis was generally synonymous with the formation and resolution of the transference neurosis. This was the idealized essence of analyzability and the sine qua non of the analytic process.

Introduction

The transference retained central therapeutic importance because it repeated and recapitulated the patient's infantile conflicts, fantasies, traumas, and object relations. The transference was not simply a form of memory, but a compromise fantasy formation, derivative of unconscious infantile conflict and trauma. As a result of interpretation, transference fantasy became the battleground for unconscious infantile conflict and the vehicle for eventual mastery. This repetition-reproduction was a new edition of the past, unconscious and disguised, and still dependent on an analytic inferential process to be understood. Memories were not always uncovered or recovered, and just what was being repeated in the transference had to be reconstructed in relation to the patient's life and neurosis. There proved to be no simple relationship between the adult neurosis, the transference neurosis, and the infantile neurosis, and all were subject to reconstruction.

Nevertheless, transference carried the greatest sense of conviction for both the patient and the analyst. Since the conflicts were revived and resolved in the living interaction of the analytic situation, the transference was the matrix for the cognitive and emotional experience of insight, and for the continued working through of interpretation. The transference had the immediacy and the impact of the here-and-now rather than the there-and-then of the dim and distant past. For those analysts for whom only transference interpretations were truly mutative, reconstruction might even be viewed as serving resistance. A reconstructive focus became an escape from current transference conflict to intellectualized preoccupation with the past. If reconstruction then was assumed to increase resistance, that resistance would be presumed to impede the analysis of transference. The psychoanalytic situation would only be a new object encounter if the transference repetition was not recognized as such, a derivative repetition of the past and a transfer from the past to the present. Reconstruction could successfully undermine or overcome resistance, and the infantile sources of resistance could be readily overlooked. Analysis could be narrowly defined solely in terms of the formation and analytic resolution of a transference neurosis. This resolution actually could not be accomplished by transference analysis alone, without genetic interpretation and reconstruction of infantile traumas and the infantile neurosis. Freud's writings simultaneously emphasized the continuing importance of reconstruction; he never endorsed a technical position attending only to the transference.

It seems apparent that analysts utilize and depend on reconstruction even where there is no such explicit acknowledgment. The analytic process requires reconstruction in order for there to be an understanding and resolution of transference repetition, an unconscious perpetuation of childhood conflicts and fixations. It is necessary to have working models of the patient's childhood, some coherent idea of the patient's main object relationships, important identifications, and the central experiences which had an enduring impact on the patient's life. To grow up with an alcoholic mother, or a single mother and a divorced, distant father, or with juvenile diabetes—all will demand a process of reconstruction of the patient's inner experience coordinated with the unfolding life history. Neither the patient's neurosis nor character can be understood without an appreciation of his or her childhood and the childhood patterns that have persisted and even permeated areas of the adult personality. Through the childish nature and origins of neurosis, and the ubiquitous derivatives of childhood traumas, analyst and patient are inevitably led to reconstruction in the psychoanalytic process.

Chapter Two

The Concept of Reconstruction in Psychoanalysis

Psychoanalysis is a science which develops a living history of the patient in the course of the psychoanalytic process, and reconstruction is thus an integral part of it. Points of view concerning history and psychological development influence attitudes toward reconstruction, which is related to the genetic principle and to the developmental framework of psychoanalysis. One of the most important discoveries that Freud made was to establish the importance of the past in the shaping of the person's personality ("the child is father of the man" [Wordsworth, "My Heart Leaps Up," 1807]), and childhood was immensely important for the understanding of human psychology and psychological disturbance. As a contribution to theory and a check up on it, reconstruction has always been linked to theories of pathogenesis. Symptoms and other forms of personality disturbance can be traced backward in time to the conflicts and traumas of childhood. In many respects neurotics continue to live in the past; they repeat old childhood patterns and relationships in the present; they struggle with unresolved, unconscious infantile conflicts, with the result that old battles may be fought inappropriately and repeatedly throughout the life-span. Furthermore, in the course of normal development, a series of infantile and childhood phases through adolescence are traversed, which leave their imprint on the personality. These phases and stages can be reconstructed and are inferred to be universal elements of human development. The importance of early object relations and the sequence of psychosexual phase development were initially reconstructed from adult psychoanalysis, always fortified by parallel observations of children and analytic studies in such diverse areas as anthropology, literature, and mythology.

The past left a living record in the memory and the personality structure, and Freud was fond of comparing the psychoanalytic process to archaeological investigation. The uncovering of unconscious conflicts, fantasies, and traumas was analogous to an archaeologist's uncovering of the buried past; psychoanalytic discoveries were compared to the achievements of archaeologists in drawing inferences from artefacts about life-style and social structure from ancient relics and reconstructing such aspects as religious sacrifices of bygone civilizations and cultures. From the traces left behind, a version of the past could be constructed, a concept also related to the lifting of infantile amnesia.

Reconstruction is a historical explanatory statement about the influence of the past on the patient. Points of view concerning history and psychological development influence attitudes toward reconstruction, which in turn has its own history in psychoanalysis. There have been varying periods of intense interest in reconstruction and its utilization in theory and technique, followed by periods of relative eclipse. Reconstruction had an important place in the evolution of psychoanalytic theory and technique, and in the validation of psychoanalytic hypotheses. It had a very significant role in Freud's self-analysis and was used to fill in gaps in memory (where analysis did not lift the infantile amnesia) and to correlate present and past. Reconstruction was applied, to cite specific examples, in the unravelling of screen memories (Freud, 1899), to trace the source of the germ of guilt deriving from infancy, and the origins of a travel phobia (Freud, 1896c). Patterns of ambivalence, the need for a beloved friend and hated enemy, the infantile prototypes for falling in love and of all object relationships, were discovered in Freud's self-analysis, and in his first patients, in conjunction with the utilization of reconstruction (Blum, 1977). Learning from the incorrect reconstruction of pathogenesis, represented by the seduction theory, Freud advanced to new levels of insight and to the bases of psychoanalytic theory (Ekstein and Rangell, 1961). Reconstruction both contributed to fundamental psychoanalytic formulations and emerged from correlated concepts of childhood repression, regression, and fixation.

The early aim of psychoanalytic work, for the treatment to be effective, was to lift the infantile amnesia. Repressed memories were to be brought into consciousness, and particularly memories of traumatic experience were to be reclaimed and reexamined by the mature personality. But amnesia did not always yield to memory retrieval, and recall and memory could be subjective, distorted, incomplete and out of context. Even before the undoing of infantile amnesia was relegated to a more peripheral aim in clinical psychoanalysis, the analyst would formulate and propose constructions concerning forgotten fragments of the patient's life history. The analyst utilized the patient's free associations and the totality of information supplied by the patient, "what he shows us in his transferences, from what we arrive at by interpreting his dreams and from what he betrays by his slips or *parapraxes*. All this material helps us to make constructions about what happened to him and has been forgotten as well as about what is happening in him now without his understanding it" (Freud, 1940, pp. 177–178).

As noted earlier, Freud (1937, 1939) used the terms *construction* and *reconstruction* interchangeably. For Freud, this was intrinsic to the search for historic truth and the creation of as complete and accurate a picture as possible of the patient's childhood. The patient's inner life and psychic reality were to be coordinated with his past life experience from the traces left behind. In the psychoanalytic process, the analyst inevitably found it necessary to reconstruct significant elements of the patient's past which had been repressed, combining gradual reconstruction with interpretation and clarification. Insofar as reconstruction developed a picture of the patient as a child as well as infantile object relations and the infantile neurosis, it guided and was reciprocally influenced by interpretation. Reconstruction substituted for missing memory, filled in gaps in memory, reconciled inconsistencies in what was remembered, and synthesized fragments of memory. Reconstruction was allied to the process of the registration, retrieval, and reorganization of memory; it was not only a memory surrogate, but it could facilitate memory recovery. "[I]f we have prepared everything properly, it often happens that the patient will at once confirm our construction and himself recollect the internal or external event which he had forgotten. The more exactly the construction coincides with the details of what has been forgotten the easier it will be for him to assent. On that particular matter *our* knowledge will then have become *his* knowledge as well" (Freud, 1940, p. 178).

In contemporary psychoanalysis the recovery of the repressed, especially of traumas, no longer has such preeminent importance, and reconstruction is not linked to memory alone. Reconstruction maintains the genetic and historical approach to the roots of the personality and psychopathology. But reconstruction is also an explanation and a method of integration—connecting past and present, fantasy and reality, cause and effect, and establishing a genetic and developmental and temporal sequence. Beyond uncovering and recovering the past (as in the archaeological model), and substituting for memory, reconstruction is a maturing reorganization of infantile life, contributing to structural renovation.

Greenacre (1981) distinguished between the analyst's initial educated conjectures about the patient's past and later carefully refined models of that past. She referred to the early, more intuitive and tentative formulations as constructions. These constructions would be replaced later by reconstructions based upon a wealth of analytic data and experience and informed by analytic knowledge, including knowledge of normal development and disorders similar to those of the particular patient. Constructions were in the mind of the analyst and were not really meant to be shared with the patient. Greenacre essentially followed Freud's (1940) own counsel, "But in all this we never fail to make a strict distinction between *our* knowledge and *his* knowledge. We avoid telling him at once things that we have often discovered at an early stage, and we avoid telling him the whole of what we think we have discovered" (p. 178).

Reconstruction would be presented to the patient, shared with and modified by the patient, and would become an explicit part of the psychoanalytic process. From the beginning of analytic research on the topic, however, it has been necessary to distinguish clearly between the analytic process and the process of reconstruction; between analytic work leading to reconstruction and reconstruction as a specific technical intervention; and between reconstruction as an overarching grand explanation encompassing pathogenesis and reconstruction as a partial, piecemeal explanatory proposition with changing content and connections. Clinically, reconstruction had to be distinguished from the analytic process in general, and from interpretation in particular.

Reconstruction was allied to but much broader than genetic interpretation. In a genetic interpretation the analyst might interpret a cannibalistic wish or the defense against that wish in anorexia, but reconstruction would deal with the broader issue of gratification, deprivation, consistency of nurturance, affective exchange, and oral phase traumas. Freud (1937) noted that construction (or reconstruction) tended to be subsumed under interpretation in accounts of analytic technique. " 'Interpretation' applies to something that one does to some single element of the material, such as an association or a parapraxis. But it is a 'construction' when one lays before the subject of the analysis a piece of his early history that he has forgotten" (p. 261). Reconstruction is thus distinguished from both the analyst's interpretation and the patient's actual memory. For Freud the awareness that reconstruction often did not succeed in bringing the patient to recollect the repressed was not regarded as a setback in therapy or theory. Freud (1937) asserted, "if the analysis is carried out correctly, we produce in him an assured conviction of the truth of the construction which achieves the same therapeutic result as a recaptured memory" (pp. 265–266).

The notion of an assured conviction of truth left unresolved questions about the nature of conviction and the basis for it. The "truth" was also not necessarily self-evident and invariant, especially about the more remote past, and controversy about the validity and therapeutic value of reconstruction remains (Novey, 1968). It was not clear if reconstruction was a regular feature of the analytic process, or if reconstruction was indicated only for certain patients, or under certain circumstances.

The Concept

Conviction for the analyst and conviction for the patient are separate issues, though subject to reciprocal transference–countertransference influences. The analytic reconstruction would also differ from that of an external videotape and historical report. The analytic data do not guarantee freedom from the analyst's own preconceptions, predilections, bias, censorship, and distortions, and this complicates the patient's own tendencies to omit and distort historical material. Reconstruction, like all interpretive interventions, is an approximation; it rests on analytic evidence, and is a rational, explanatory inference about the past in the context of the present analytic process, while it is at the same time "history in the making." Though reconstruction may be confirmed by external sources and data, analytic validation does not require such extra-analytic confirmation. Over the course of psychoanalytic history interest in dreams and the importance ascribed to them and to transference have influenced the history of reconstruction. Dreams were to be the royal road to the infantile unconscious, and, for the pioneer analysts, were closer to archaeological excavation of the buried past than other forms of analytic data. However, dreams were also understood within the transference, where the past was on display in the analytic situation. Conflicts were to be fought out on the battlefield of the transference, and for reconstruction there was less emphasis upon dreams and screen memories. Reconstruction could be regarded as a resistance through a flight from the present to the past, a flight from current affective conflict to contemplation of "long ago and far away." It was recognized, in the course of analytic work, that the resistance could take either direction—the past could defend against the present, the present against the past. But transference analysis gradually overshadowed reconstruction.

Interest in reconstruction has waxed and waned during different periods of psychoanalytic history, but has been particularly sensitive to theories of pathogenesis. Controversy about pathogenesis encompassed scientific and philosophical issues concerning early development and personality formation. The formulations of Adler, Jung, Klein, and the British object relations school were all tested in the analytic process with inevitable alternate reconstructions. More recently, Kohut (1971) and self psychology, structuralism, and competing theories about borderline personality (Knight, 1953; Kernberg, 1975) have converged with the contributions of Jacobson (1964) and Mahler (1971) in eliciting attention to reconstruction. The development of classical structural theory had emerged from considerations of conflict and trauma rooted in infancy, and classical theory was both buttressed and challenged by reconstructions about infancy and pathogenesis.

Although lack of empathy would replace childhood seduction as a decisive etiology in self psychology, the roles of reality and of fantasy have been recurrent problems in psychoanalysis. The evaluation of traumatic pathogenesis tended to polarize fantasy, objective and subjective views of actual experience. Patients' reports of their actual experience were first taken literally and at face value. Reports of childhood seductions, of incestuous molestation of children by parents and caregivers, were initially regarded as valid. These historical accounts by patients, and the fact that so many of the patients' associations seemed to correlate adult symptoms with childhood sexual experience, led to a particular theory of pathogenesis and mode of treatment. Freud hypothesized the existence of the "seduction theory," associated with the "cathartic method" of treatment (Breuer and Freud, 1895). Childhood seduction resulted in persisting pathogenic influences responsible for adult symptomatic disturbance. Treatment consisted of uncovering the childhood trauma from repression, lifting that trauma into conscious awareness, releasing strangulated affects associated with the trauma, and allowing the patient to establish and restore cognitive connections between the traumatic past and the present. The original traumatic situation was connected to current situations and symptoms which represented or were derivatives of the trauma. Aspects of present life might repeat, defend against, or evoke the traumatic experience of the past. *"Hysterics suffer mainly from reminiscences"* (Breuer and Freud, 1895), and these reminiscences are representative of repressed and forgotten childhood experiences which could be later remembered or reconstructed in the treatment process. When the seduction theory was abandoned (Freud, 1892–1899), the controversy between fact and fiction, actual experience versus fantasy and myth, came to the fore and has periodically reappeared ever since. The abandonment of the seduction theory and the realization that patients' narratives about their own early history could not be simply accepted as accurate would lead to an ongoing tension between factual and fictional history, between fantasy and reality in mental life. This controversy has taken different forms and is currently often categorized as narrative versus historical truth (Spence, 1982).

Some analysts felt psychoanalysis would be concerned primarily with unconscious fantasy elaboration, with the overall importance of unconscious intrapsychic conflict and fantasy. Actual trauma and real experience became relatively peripheral for some analysts, either unobtainable or relatively unimportant, or both. The traumatic event or the specific traumatic situation gave way to new directions in addition to fantasy considerations. The event disappeared into both fantasy and patterns. Shock trauma would be absorbed into pathogenic impressions, patterns, and universal fantasies. The actual traumatic event, Kris (1956c) proposed, merged with pathogenic patterns of developmental strain, and specific traumatic shock situations need not be and probably could not be accurately reconstructed. In contrast, Greenacre (1956) continued to emphasize specific external events and fantasies that "have been given a special strength, form, and pressure for repetition through having been confirmed by external events" (p. 440). Contemporary proponents of reconstruction combine the different views and want to know the events (what happened), the inner experience and meaning of the events, and their immediate and distant consequences, to the extent that this can be ascertained. Denial and confusion cannot be clarified without connection to the reality that was denied.

The early emphasis which Freud gave to reconstruction was continued by Greenacre (1956, 1980), Lewin (1955), and other analysts (e.g., Reider, 1953; Rosen, 1953; Frank, 1969; Kris Study Group, 1971; Blum, 1977, 1980) who were particularly oriented toward childhood and toward genetic and developmental considerations. In many of these studies, a reconstruction was an explanatory proposition that established genetic connections and developmental sequences for the adult analytic material under investigation, although reconstruction was also related to the process of working through. As time went on, it was possible to discern an increasing emphasis on synthesis and integration of the inner life and history not previously available to the patient.

Child analysts were especially sensitive to the importance of the child's actual experience with parents and peers, and the role of the environment was never entirely subordinate to the transference. Since the child often did not develop a transference neurosis, transference was of less significance in the child analytic process than in adult analysis. However, the emphasis on the importance of fantasy partially derived from Freud's (1892–1899) recognition that the seduction theory was oversimplified and incorrect. Clinical and theoretical interest turned from individual, accidental experience and trauma to the universals of development. This led to the discovery of the Oedipus complex and the subsequent formulation of the lidibo theory.

The fact that Freud disbelieved some patients' reports of actual childhood seduction and came to recognize the significance of fantasy did not mean that he had discarded the reality of traumatic child abuse. The fantasies of trauma and the fantasy elaboration of actual trauma required explanation, one which also entailed reconstruction. What was reconstructed was no longer likely to be the patient as passive victim, but the patient as an active agent in the shaping of both fantasy and his own experience. The patient produced his own internally generated fantasies, and these fantasies had a complex relationship to an external reality distorted by projection and transference, often influenced by the patient's own behavior. The fantasies of trauma (e.g., childhood seduction) also defended against the child's own seductiveness and infantile masturbation. Reconstruction moved from seduction experience to fantasy and back to experience; it led from the fantasy of trauma in some cases to the ubiquity of fantasy. The reconstructed past pointed to universal experience, not of external seduction, but of autoerotic activity. Passive victimization, true at times and in degree, was replaced by a more comprehensive view of the child's development and the child's defense against awareness of his own forbidden motives, attitudes, and actions. When trauma did occur, the trauma intensified and activated preexisting conflicts and fantasies as well as traumas, so that there was a condensation of fantasy and reality. No single event was likely to be the first link in a causal chain, with overdetermination at every point in the sequence. Any childhood experience could be understood as being codetermined by internal and external reality.

The decisive turn from the significance of real

trauma to the inner life and the significance of fantasy, was a landmark in the history of human thought. The patient's account of his own life experience was recognized as subject to all manner of subjective distortions. The conscious historical account, elaborated in the treatment process, was not much more reliable than a direct psychiatric anamnesis and was rife with gaps, distortions, inconsistencies, fabrications, and confabulations. Bias was inevitably built into the patient's awareness and understanding of his own historical experience and that very bias cast doubt on the recovery of memories and the validity of reconstruction. Memory itself was so often fragmentary and fragmented, how could reconstruction fill in gaps in such unreliable memories? Memory itself was subject to defensive distortion and all the problems of memory, its registration and retrieval, influenced attitudes toward reconstruction. Perhaps there were no memories of the past, in effect, only subjective and edited recollections. When he considered the uncertain, blurred boundary between memory and fantasy construction, Freud (1899) pondered whether what seemed to be remembered was really recreated afresh in the present. He then proposed:

> It may indeed be questioned whether we have any memories at all *from* our childhood: memories *relating* to our childhood may be all that we possess. Our childhood memories show us our earliest years not as they were but as they appeared at the later periods when the memories were aroused. In these periods of arousal, the childhood memories did not, as people are accustomed to say, *emerge*; they were *formed* at that time. And a number of motives, with no concern for historical accuracy, had a part in forming them, as well as in the selection of the memories themselves [p. 322].

Was not all memory really screen memory? The past was filtered through the distorting lens of the present and could only be seen through a glass darkly. Though questioning memory might have led to reconstruction as a reorganization and correction of memory, rather than mainly a substitution for what could not be retrieved through remembering, reconstruction was regarded as more likely to be unreliable. It seemed that many analysts, forewarned by Freud's early experience of having been seduced by tales of childhood seduction, tended to deemphasize the recall of incestuous trauma and then of traumatic memories in general. The devaluation of reconstruction was associated with increasing analytic interest in the personal myth (Kris, 1956b) and the analysis of unconscious conflict and fantasy as particularly expressed in the transference. Reconstruction might be associated with inexact interpretation and with the imposition of analytic myth on personal myth. The analyst should not distort or rewrite history in the process of reconstruction, but might nevertheless do so. Controversy concerning the validity of reconstruction has been present since the first incorrect reconstruction of the seduction theory of pathogenesis.

In the main, the importance of both trauma and beneficial experience has continued to be acknowledged, but the significance accorded to actual experience in treatment and training has varied considerably. After Freud's death, for about 35 years, reconstruction tended to fade from the analytic educational scene, hardly articulated in courses on technique, in supervision, and in clinical case seminars and reports. Its technical use, however, probably continued without being specifically identified and labeled.

The rise of defense analysis again, after Freud's death and World War II, tended to obscure the role of reconstruction, but paradoxically returned with attention to such defenses as the denial of reality, undoing, and identification. The role of identification with real objects as a defense and considerations of the role of identification in structure formation and development, in the long run, would bring renewed consideration of reconstruction. The swing of the pendulum back toward reconstruction was related to its utilization in establishing prototypical patterns of childhood; for example, object relations and identifications, defense and adaptation. Reconstruction was also implicit in reconsideration of the infantile neurosis as prototype or precursor of the adult neurosis and the transference neurosis. The adult neurosis was not a replica or direct linear derivative of the infantile neurosis. The infantile neurosis had been transformed during development and was in itself a reconstruction in adult analysis (A. Freud, 1970).

Advances in psychoanalysis and other areas would also have an important influence upon reconstruction. While reconstruction took into account constitutional factors as in the formulation of libido theory and in the innate equipment of the ego (Hartmann, 1939; A. Freud and Burlingham, 1944), reconstruction received fresh impetus from renewed attention to the nurture side of nature–nurture. This duality of the constitutional and the experiential was related to reality and fantasy but was quite different from both. Psychoanalysis had always dealt with both the outside and the inside of the psyche and their coordinates and correlations. Freud (1916–1917) had early developed the notion of a complemental series to take into account the reciprocal interaction of nature and nurture. The innate and the environment, the accidental and the universal, all have their place in psychoanalytic theory and practice. Hartmann (1939) paid new attention to the importance of ego endowment and of the environment. The rise of ego psychology which followed after World War II was to be associated with a shift from universal fantasies and defenses to more general considerations of function, development, adaptation, and mastery.

Earlier studies of drive development gave way to studies of structural development which allowed for the articulation of reconstruction from adult analysis with reconstruction in child analysis and now with direct child observation. Child observation and developmental research doubtless stimulated reciprocal interest in reconstruction. The psychosexual developmental framework was supplemented by the important additions of the complex intertwining of ego development and object relations. The studies of many analysts, such as Jacobson (1964), Spitz (1965), Winnicott (1965), and particularly Mahler, Pine, and Bergman (1975), along with Mahler's theory of separation-individuation, expanded knowledge of early development and demonstrated anew the fundamental importance of the earliest relationship between child and caregiver. Object relations, important in psychoanalysis before the formulation of the libido theory, again came to the fore. The genetic and developmental perspectives were so informative and suggestive that they seemed at times not only to enrich but to overshadow other theoretical and clinical dimensions. Particularly valuable in the developmental studies was the renewed effort to trace the subtle and complex interrelationships between the innate and the environmental, the influence of constitution upon experience, and both upon subsequent development. Focus on the process of separation-individuation also stimulated and rekindled interest in the preverbal period and its analytic reconstruction. Controversy about preverbal inferences and reconstruction quickly became intense.

Psychoanalysis had always been concerned with the unconscious and developmental consequences of experience, not merely with experience itself. Experiences such as trauma were important because of the persisting impact upon subsequent development and upon the adult personality. Historical facts, even if they could be ascertained, have little meaning in themselves, that is, without their psychological assimilation and subjective interpretation. What was important was sometimes only the intrapsychic meaning of the facts; that these meanings were also inevitably a function of the facts tended to be disregarded. In the extreme form of this position, any reconstruction of the past was suspect. Only those observations made directly in the analytic situation could be taken as having a relative degree of reality and accuracy. It was as if the analyst would only accept what he had directly seen and heard in the analytic situation.

This point of view, which depreciates the relevance of factual history and real life experience, does not emerge in any of Freud's own clinical examples. Psychoanalysis revealed a whole hierarchy of motives and conflicts outside of the patient's awareness. These conflicts were not only unconscious but infantile in origin. Unconscious conflicts and fantasies could be traced and placed in their infantile context. Freud (1905) and Dora understood her experiences of seduction by her father's friend, Herr K; but Freud also wanted her to understand the inner truth of her own seductive wishes and derivative conflicts. Freud not only reconstructed the circumstances surrounding the relatively recent suicide note which had precipitated Dora's being brought to him for treatment, but also her infantile masturbation and primal scene experience. The victim's position of having been exposed to attempted seduction also disguised her own seductiveness and masturbation.

In this pioneering and pathfinding encounter, Freud (1905) did not treat the patient's real seduction experiences as fantasy nor her fantasies as reality. Distortions and reversals can occur in either direction by treating reality as fantasy or fantasy as reality. Reconstruction is not concerned with simple historical or factual events of the past but rather with the inner meaning and consequences of that past as it was also shaped by the patient.

The historical facts are not disregarded as, for example, with respect to Dora's feeling like a bartered bride, offered to Herr K by her father in exchange for Frau K. The web of familial and extrafamilial intrigue and collusion has meaning in terms of deception, seduction, lack of protection, and Dora's unconscious intensified, defensive, and regressive longing for her mother's love and comfort. The circumstances of Dora's life and their unconscious significance are crucial to analytic reconstruction. And this reconstruction "upwards" of the present is dynamically related to Dora's transference fantasies and to the genetic prototypes of transference repetition in the here-and-now of the analytic situation. Reconstruction contributes to and is part of the genetic and developmental explanation of what is being repeated in the transference.

Reconstruction is synergistic with transference and yet a contrapuntal expression of the distant past rather than the immediate here-and-now. Transference is always present and often dramatically visible and audible in the analytic situation. For many analysts, the here-and-now of transference seems to be more tangible than the there-and-then of reconstruction, which is an explanatory substitute for the more remote and distant past and a reflection of it.

However, without reconstruction the transference itself might be viewed primarily in terms of the current doctor–patient relationship and interaction, rather than as a revival of infantile life. Transference is a new edition of the conflicts, fantasies, and relationships of childhood (Freud, 1905), and transference retains an essentially childish character. It cannot be fully understood, therefore, without analysis of its defensive distortions, regressive alterations, and developmental changes. Transference and reconstruction have a reciprocal relationship to each other, since transference leads to genetic interpretation and reconstruction, and reconstruction potentiates transference analysis. The analytic data upon which reconstruction is based are related to transference, and the reconstruction itself is subject to transference investment and remodeling in the analytic process.

This polarization of reconstruction versus transference, rather than the continuous interrelationship of past and present, was also related to an idealization of the transference. It was as if the transference reproduced the entire history of the patient in a form accessible to the analyst without genetic exposition and reconstruction. The patient might repeat intense early sibling rivalry in the transference in the form of feeling that the analyst was bored and preferred other patients, jealousy of the analyst and of the analyst's interest in his other patients, his family, and colleagues. The traumatic elements in the patient's experience of the birth of a sibling in his own infancy might well be repeated in the transference, but in disguised form. The patient, becoming aware of envy, jealousy, rivalry, and identification with the current rival, does not unravel the genetic roots of his or her conflicts. Discovery of rivalry and jealousy in the analytic situation and the transference does not in itself lift repression and undo infantile amnesia, and does not overcome the isolation of past and present. The entire constellation of the events, reactions, and patterns following from the birth of the sibling require reconstruction in addition to the analysis of transference, defense, and all the other significant ingredients of the psychoanalytic process. The patient who falls in love with the analyst may recognize that it is irrational, ambivalent, and possessive, but will not easily recognize the incestuous and truly childish character of the erotic transference. The influence of the patient's infancy upon his current life can then be more fully appreciated. From the viewpoint that favors reconstruction, psychic reality and external reality have reciprocal interweaving influences, and the inner life and inner meaning cannot be understood without its external coordinates and without understanding unconscious conflict, temporal and developmental sequence, cause, and effect. The reconstruction would not attempt to deal with, nor would it necessarily resemble, what an external observer would note if he were to scrutinize the child at the time of the sibling's birth. But the reconstruction would certainly take into account the fact that the child's psychological reactions were in response to the sibling's birth and the altered parent–child and parental relationships and family dynamics.

This illumination of the past within the present analytic work is what Freud (1937) had in mind when he addressed the issue of reconstruction both as a technique and as a goal of analysis. The reconstruction of the patient's childhood from the traces left behind was the goal of analysis. Experiences such as the birth of a sibling impacted upon the individual's life and were part of his authentic and unique life history. The childhood situation could be reconstructed in a form which approximated the complexity of the actual experience and the internal psychological meanings of that experience. Freud (1937) stated, " 'Up to your nth year you regarded yourself as the sole and unlimited possessor of your mother; then came another baby and brought you grave disillusionment. Your mother left you for some time, and even after her reappearance she was never again devoted to you exclusively. Your feelings towards your mother became ambivalent, your father gained a new importance for you,' . . . and so on" (p. 261).

The relationship of reconstruction to the actual or factual past in psychoanalysis was further alluded to when Freud (1937) noted that every delusion has a grain of truth. This meant that delusion, and indeed all fantasy, could not be fully understood without taking into account the nidus of reality contained within. An obese adult might have unconscious fantasies of devouring objects and of being devoured, but it would be important to know whether there were actual experiences of early separation and loss, of infantile feeding disturbance. The whole quality of early object relations would be relevant, and the analyst would want to know whether food was used by either parent or child as an ambivalent communication to express or withhold love, to reward or punish, or to represent dependence or autonomy. The Rat Man's fantasies of anal penetration and torment would be more closely connected to a complex set of issues, including childhood illness and sibling death, childhood seduction, intestinal parasites and their treatment with enemas and laxatives (Freud, 1909). The transference meaning of the current analytic treatment would be correlated with the genetic meanings of medical care, childhood voyeurism and exhibitionism, parental demands and expectations, and identification with parents who are social climbers and preoccupied with money and status. The homosexual fantasies in the transference of the Rat Man would then have to be understood in relation to his conflicts activated and engendered by his army experience, his current problems and preoccupations with marriage, and a whole network of connected fantasies and experiences going back to infancy. There is no simple relationship between the Rat Man's rat preoccupations and fantasies and his life experience. Contemporary reconstruction would encompass far more than the equivalent of memory, but might establish the preoedipal affective attunement and temperament of the patient and his or her subjective experience of the climate, context, and content of the parent–infant relationship; it would encompass the antecedents and outcome of oedipal conflict.

The reconstructed past as obtained in analysis has been retrieved, recreated, and created. It is a world which did not exist intrapsychically in its original form (the ur experience as it were) on the same level of integration and developmental sophistication. The child does not have the language, concepts, affects, or integration of the adult. A reconstruction is an analytic synthesis which could not be directly observed and could not be formulated by the external observer, lacking the intrapsychic analytic data. The reconstructed world of the past comes to life in the present, is animated by the present, and is dynamically related to the present. The analytically determined past is history evolving, codetermined by fantasy and reality. It is remodeled in the course of analytic work by both patient and analyst. It is a past of multiple perspectives and many dimensions, brought into a cohesive and coherent fit that offers that most meaningful and comprehensive integration. In the course of analytic work, a particular facet of the past is constructed in relation to the patient's present personality and problems, and the dynamic issues in the transference. This construction of the past, whether of childhood seduction, illness, loss, or special identification, is more like a developing, ever more detailed and documented, analytically transformed life study than a palpable, static archaeological relic. The past is perceived differently in different phases of psychoanalysis and in different phases of life. Reconstruction gains in clarity and objectivity as the analytic process proceeds but is never "what really happened," as might be proposed by external observers or historians. And they would not necessarily agree about the observations or the interpretation of history.

Reconstruction is not simply arbitrary, capricious, or subjective as in any narrative reader's attribution of meaning. Psychoanalytic reconstruction is instead based upon scientific principles of causality, coherence, and logic, parsimonious explanation, articulation with known developmental knowledge, and the best fit with the given analytic data. Alternative reconstructions are repeatedly tested in the analytic process, revised and updated as the analysis deepens. There are special problems concerning the process of reconstruction within and as part of the total analytic process, the use of reconstruction as an explanatory framework for interpretation, the timing and readiness for reconstruction, and the content and depth of reconstruction in the essentially verbal analytic dialogue. The reconstruction of developmental sequence and developmental disharmony and disturbance, as well as achievements and mastery, has superseded the earlier, narrower reconstruction of psychosexual phases and instinctual fixation and regression. With all the complex difficulties of developmental phase considerations, currently reconstruction attempts to encompass the challenges and conflicts associated with childhood development and with the subsequent phases of the life cycle. It is highly probable that every analyst develops a reconstructed model of each patient's childhood and development which forms a rough template for the comprehension of the adult and infantile neurosis. The patient's infantile features and fantasies invite the analyst's construction and compel their gradual analytic reconstruction. The reconstruction of the patient's unconscious fantasies and conflicts is intrinsic to the analysis of intrapsychic conflict and the understanding of the patient's personality development and disorder. The interaction of the intrapsychic with the familial, social, and cultural environment, the patient's self and object representations, and identifications, all converge in the process of reconstruction. Different analysts, patients, and analytic schools approach these issues with significant variation, but common interests, for example, in pathogenesis or in the development of special skills and sublimations, foster reconstruction in theory and practice.

An early example of a reconstruction of Freud, based upon dream analysis, and taking into account both intra-psychic and familial considerations, was recorded by Kardiner (1977, p. 75).

> Oberndorf got to be on bad terms with Freud on the very first day of his analysis, because he came prepared with a dream, which he related in the very first hour. The dream was as follows: He was riding in a carriage pulled by two horses, one of which was white, and the other black. They were going to some unknown destination. Traveling to an unknown destination as an opening dream in analysis is not infrequent. But this particular dream happened, rightly or wrongly, to hit upon one of Oberndorf's apparent weak spots, because it was Freud's interpretation that he, Oberndorf, could never marry because he didn't know whether to choose a white woman or a black woman, and so he was in a quandary. He was not married then, nor did he ever marry, and he was a Southerner. He was born in Atlanta, Georgia, and had been raised by a black "mammy."

Unfortunately, the reconstruction infuriated the patient, and after haggling about the dream for months, Freud discontinued the analysis. Nevertheless, this remains an extraordinary evocation of the problems of multiple mothering in relation to unconscious conflict and character disorder at a time when such problems were hardly recognized. The example may also serve as a caution against premature interpretation and reconstruction which intensifies resistance.

Chapter Three

The Reconstruction of Trauma in Clinical Psychoanalysis

The early formulations of the psychoanalytic theory of psychopathology were cast in a traumatic mold. Freud's initial therapeutic efforts led to memories of childhood traumas which Breuer and Freud (1895) believed were essentially experiences of sexual abuse prior to the age of 8. Freud became convinced that the sexual experiences described to him by his patients had occurred in their childhood. In addition to the involvement of parents in infantile seductions, he also spoke of teachers and nursemaids, servants and siblings. The siblings who had already been seduced by an adult tended to seduce younger siblings, an early example of the repetition of trauma, identification with the abuser or aggressor, and the tendency for seduction trauma to occur in a pattern and setting of a seductive familial atmosphere. Freud (1896a, p. 169) concurrently noted constitutional factors in the choice of hysteria or obsessional symptoms. The traumatic experience of the past had enduring influence on personality

This chapter is a revised version of "The Concept of Reconstruction of Trauma," originally published in *The Reconstruction of Trauma: Its Significance in Clinical Work* (1986), ed. Arnold Rothstein. Madison, CT: International Universities Press.

organization and function. Trauma could be uncovered or reconstructed, and reconstruction figured prominently in Freud's self-analysis. Reconstruction is intrinsic to analytic technique (even when not labeled as such) and important for the development and testing of analytic theory.

Distinguishing between the causes and consequences of trauma, Breuer and Freud (1895) described both the quantitative factor in the etiology of trauma and the defensive repression of the traumatic experience. Childhood sexual abuse possibly produced no effect at the time of the traumatic event, but later imparted to the memory of the trauma the functional capacity of the current situation. The importance of childhood trauma in pathogenesis and personality development gave rise to the well-known dictum, *"Hysterics suffer mainly from reminiscences"* (Breuer and Freud, 1895, p. 7). The abreaction of repressed trauma with its strangulated affects was the first theory of therapy and had a lasting impact on subsequent theories of pathogenesis and treatment. Furst (1967) aptly emphasized that trauma was a multifaceted problem and the early formulations foreshadowed the later theoretical concepts.

Freud proceeded to the understanding that many of the "memories" of childhood seduction were in actuality fantasies, a revolutionary realization which led to the discovery of infantile sexuality and the Oedipus complex. He later unequivocally stated, "the position can be shown to be that the childhood experiences constructed or remembered in analysis are sometimes indisputably false and sometimes equally certainly correct, and in most cases compounded of truth and falsehood" (Freud, 1916–1917, p. 367). The "seduction theory" represented an exclusive traumatic pathogenesis, a theory that was recognized as being drastically oversimplified and inaccurate. The seduction theory was discarded but the pathogenic significance of seduction and other forms of trauma was retained.

Actual trauma, infantile sexuality, and libido theory were complementary in the same way that external and internal factors, nature and nurture, were always considered to coexist, coact, and to a degree were codeterminants of both vulnerability and disorder. Freud (1914a) remarked: "*disposition* exaggerates impressions which otherwise have been completely commonplace and have had no effect, so that they become traumas giving rise to stimulations and fixations; while *experiences* awaken factors in the disposition which, without them, might have long remained dormant and perhaps never have developed" (p. 18).

Freud (1920a, p. 29) described "any excitations from outside which are powerful enough to break through the protective shield" as traumatic. The concept of trauma then further evolved to considerations of ego helplessness in the face of danger which could thus occur at virtually any period of life. Ego immaturity predisposed the individual to helplessness. The concept of a protective shield or external stimulus barrier was also gradually altered and may now be regarded as antiquated. The protective shield does not describe the neonate's screening and selection of internal as well as external stimuli, with innate receptive as well as protective processes (Esman, 1983; Shapiro and Stern, 1989). The infant's protective endowment is supplemented by and coordinated with the mother's auxiliary ego function and holding environment; the caregiver stimulates, modulates, and organizes while being reciprocally stimulated and organized by the infant (A. Freud, 1970; Mahler and McDevitt, 1980).

As Strachey notes in his Editor's Introduction to "Inhibitions, Symptoms and Anxiety," Freud (1926a) expanded his view of trauma beyond external overstimulation. Strachey says, "the essence of [a traumatic situation] is an experience of helplessness on the part of the ego in the face of accumulation of excitation, whether of external or internal origin" (p. 81). Trauma could perhaps cause permanent damage, "with an increase of stimulus too powerful to be dealt with or worked off in the normal way, and this must result in permanent disturbances of the manner in which energy operates" (Freud, 1916–1917, p. 275). The intensity of the potential trauma would be weighed against the strength of the ego and particularly of ego defense, after defense mechanisms were developmentally available.

Moving beyond only quantitative considerations, Freud (1926a) noted displacement from the danger situation itself to the determinant of the danger in terms of loss of object and the object's love, care, and protection. While birth and separation from a mother were the prototypes for later anxiety situations, there was no birth trauma (Rank, 1924). There was a developmental sequence of potential traumas due to loss of the object, loss of the object's love, castration threats, and superego condemnation. All potential traumatic situations involved considerations of the strength and resources of the ego and a complemental series of internal and external factors. The question of whether anxiety was a cause or a consequence of the traumatic situation was not resolved. Trauma was clearly not a singular factor of sexual overstimulation and not necessarily due to the drives (both sexual and aggressive), ego fragility, or any simple explanation. The etiology of trauma is typically overdetermined and Freud (1939) discussed two effects of trauma, positive and negative, stating:

> The former are attempts to bring the trauma into operation once again—that is, to remember the forgotten experience or, better still, to make it real, to experience a repetition of it anew, or, even if it was only an early emotional relationship, to revive it in an analogous relationship with someone else. We summarize these efforts under the name

of "fixations" to the trauma and as a "compulsion to repeat". . . .

The negative reactions follow the opposite aim: that nothing of the forgotten traumas shall be remembered and nothing repeated [pp. 75–76].

While the seduction theory first emphasized the role of libidinal factors and of fathers alone, Freud (1933, p. 120) later found the preoedipal mother behind the figure of the seductive oedipal father, and also noted that it was the mother who might alternate seduction with prohibition of masturbation. Seduction fantasies themselves came to be initially understood as defending against infantile masturbation.

The Wolf Man's case (Freud, 1918) is a model for the clinical reconstruction of trauma and has had a significant influence on psychoanalytic concepts of trauma, the primal scene, and reconstruction (Blum, 1977). The Wolf Man's exposure to the parental primal scene at 5:00 P.M. one afternoon, when he was 18 months of age, has long been the model of sexual seduction and the traumatic effect for the child of being a witness to the primal scene. This was a case of shock trauma which shattered the Wolf Man's sexual development, had profound effects in the form of symptoms and character pathology, and left the Wolf Man fixated to the primal scene and defenses against it. This was evident in his sexual interests, in his character and symptoms, and his feeling that the world was hidden from him behind a veil. He was intent on looking, prohibited from seeing, and repeated in fantasy and action derivatives of the primal scene. The fantasy elaboration and distortion of the primal scene as a sadomasochistic struggle and as resulting in castration demonstrated the importance of the unconscious meaning of the traumatic experience. The unconscious fantasy and associated conflicts became as significant clinically and theoretically as the quantitative overstimulation (or more so).

As a case of shock trauma, the Wolf Man's primal scene was, in many respects, a continuation of the seduction theory of neurosogenesis. The elaborate case report, which both enriched and complicated psychoanalytic theory, conclusively demonstrated that Freud did not abandon seduction trauma as an etiological factor, and that trauma coexisted with conflict in the etiology of a severe childhood and adult neurosis. He considered alternative reconstructions of the primal scene, including issues of reality and fantasy, phase specificity, and preoedipal, deferred, and retrospective trauma.

In addition to the single shock of the parental primal scene, there was vulnerability from the early pneumonia and a concurrent malaria. The Wolf Man's father was manic-depressive, and his mother hypochondriacal. There was additional seduction by his sister, exposure to animal copulation and castration, to separation from his parents, and direct castration threats. When one considers the wealth of material, the intricate and interlacing sets of experience, the single afternoon's exposure to the primal scene is clearly set within a background of stress and strain, in a special developmental and cultural setting. The primal scene trauma can also be understood as both a screen memory and an explanatory metaphor for a far more complicated pathogenesis.

The specific causative shock that was traumatic and dramatic, caught the popular imagination (e.g., in literature and the theater). Shock trauma, for example, seduction, could also be a seductively simple explanation, given overdetermination and long-standing pathogenic patterns, as in child abuse and neglect. Reconstruction substituted for missing memory, revised and synthesized memory fragments, and placed the traumatic experience in its dynamic and developmental context with restoration of temporal and genetic sequence. Greenacre (1981) also distinguished between the analyst's tentative and uncommunicated construction and the analyst's reconstruction as a clinical intervention which is shared with the patient. Analyst and patient may share in the process of reconstruction.

At the same time shock trauma had to be rescued and differentiated from any adverse experience and noxious developmental strain. Strain refers to long-acting pathogenic determinants, distorted patterns of development, and also to predisposition and to vulnerability. Strain may potentiate shock trauma, and shock inevitably creates strain in its aftermath. Strain may appear to have only deferred or relatively silent effects, unlike the overwhelming impact of shock trauma. Strain trauma is a useful metaphor, but may be misleading if confused with shock trauma and its concomitant ego collapse and expectable sequential consequences.

Infantile traumas are ubiquitous and multiple, and may have additive or cumulative effects as Breuer and Freud (1895) and Khan (1963) proposed. Cumulative trauma tends to merge with strain, and we have to consider whether additive effects may not engender consequences similar to those of shock trauma. By definition, the nature of trauma is overwhelming. It temporarily overthrows the ego's defenses and adaptive resources, and always has the immediate effect of producing helplessness, automatic anxiety, and obligatory regression to the archaic ego (or pre-ego) function followed by obligatory repetitive phenomena. There are tendencies to repeat the trauma in thought (flashbacks, obsessions, etc.), feeling, action, in nightmares, play, symptoms, and in therapeutic transference. The repetitions may be in the service of mastery or may fail with the return of traumatic anxiety and the provocation of new noxious or traumatic experience. Trauma, initially, injures ego regulation of impulse and affects, the control of regression, higher level defenses and capacities, and self-esteem, but the long-range effects are highly variable. Much depends upon the extent and duration of traumatization and the state of helplessness and overwhelming anxiety equivalent to terror. The resilience of the personality and the capacity of the ego to reverse and regulate regression, to regain stability, and to limit or contain pathogenic aftereffects, are major factors in the mastery of trauma. Damage control is impeded by repression, regression, and repeated injury or failure. Since trauma is centrally associated with unconscious conflict and fantasy, the persistent vulnerability to the reactivation of earlier trauma is relevant to pathogenic conflict and defense and to all symptom and character disturbance. Severe trauma leaves its imprint upon the personality, and such a traumatized individual is never the same person again.

Verbalization is usually impossible in the acute traumatic situation, and motility may be frozen, frantic, or chaotic. Denial is inevitably used to defend against external trauma, though it may be superseded by other defenses. Initial psychic disorganization is followed by a post-traumatic organizing effect which absorbs much of the traumatic residua, impacts on the present personality, and influences further development. I infer that the definition of trauma does not rely upon the notion of strain or screen trauma, cumulative or retrospective trauma, deferred or posthumous trauma. The traumatic situation has immediate effects as well as more distant and enduring consequences (A. Freud, 1967).

The death of a child, the death of a parent in childhood, traumatic accidents and injuries, and life-threatening illness in the patient or a loved one, all these are examples of the importance of actual traumatic experience. Anniversary reactions are often examples of timed and tamed recurrences of childhood traumas (Pollock, 1970). Trauma may encompass radical change in the self and object world, leading to confusion and discontinuity, a "great divide" in the patient's life which such anniversary reactions attempt to bridge and integrate (Blum, 1980,

1983). Among the factors that have to be taken into account are the innate endowment of the child, including drive and ego attributes, constitutional dispositions and temperament, unusual sensitivities or strengths, and the phase of development at the time of traumas. Then again, the total psychic situation must be considered, including the reactions of parents or caretakers at the time, and the influence of antecedent and later developmental phases, fantasies, and experience upon each other. The traumatic experience as such may only be recoverable and defined in analysis at a later time.

The early psychoanalytic case histories (especially that of the Wolf Man) introduced many different conceptions connected with trauma, and in the course of time, tended to blur the distinction between adverse, pathogenic influences in general and trauma in particular (A. Freud, 1967). The importance of constitution and vulnerability takes into account the fact that what is traumatic for one child may not be traumatic for another child. In addition, there is the fact that what is traumatic for an individual at one point in development may not be traumatic at another developmental phase (Rangell, 1967). Given pathogenic patterns and a whole range of pathogenic experience, it may be very difficult or impossible to isolate a discrete traumatic experience, delineate its immediate meaning for the patient, and trace its developmental consequences. Actual beatings, beating fantasies, blows of fate and misfortune, and self-inflicted injuries may have very complicated relationships. The search for the "original trauma" or the specific shock trauma tended to be reductionist in its approach to the complexity and overdetermination of psychic life (Neubauer, 1967). The awareness of overdetermination and complexity has moved contemporary psychoanalysis away from the model of the shock trauma, a model which has been expanded and modified but which has not been entirely superseded. The model now always includes associated strain, unconscious conflicts, and the unconscious meaning of the trauma. Traumatic experiences also are determinants of subsequent relationships and identifications which have a spiraling impact upon the patient's life.

One of the major aspects of defense against trauma is denial of a terrifying reality. Denial, repression, isolation, and the whole defensive constellation found with a forgotten traumatic experience is indicative of the importance of the working through of the external as well as the internal coordinates of the trauma. Often, as in the case of childhood seduction or aggressive abuse, there is shared denial with the parents; conscious and unconscious threats against disclosure; fear of the consequences of disclosure for all members of the family; and cues and directives prohibiting recollection and discussion. After the seduction, parent and child may act as though nothing had happened. The silent complicity of the spouse in parent–child abuse is well known, and the conspiracy of silence may continue in the analytic situation if the trauma is treated only as though it were a fantasy. There are many distortions and half-truths; it is important to understand to what degree they were synthesized by the child and how they were also formed and fed by the environment. One recalls here Dora's suicide note (Freud, 1905) which followed her father's denial, Herr K's denial, and attempts to convince Dora that their seductive behavior was all a figment of her prurient imagination. Even early on in the Dora case Freud noted her own sexual interests but did not treat her stories of seduction as simply fantasy or fabrication. Freud not only reconstructed her overhearing the primal scene in childhood and her adolescent seduction by and of Herr and Frau K, but also commented on her reliability as an observer and reporter.

The parent's denial may be borrowed along with his or her guilt; that is to say, the child may choose defenses on the model of the parent and identify with the parent's self-recrimination, taking on the parental guilt. The patient may reexperience in the analytic relationship the prohibition against remembering and reflecting and the old confusion about what really happened, if it indeed happened at all. Doubt and confusion about fantasy and reality may be fostered by parental attitudes, which may have to be laboriously reconstructed (Kramer, 1983). Such confusion compounded by denial, doubt, and ego regression may lead to impairments in both judgment and reality testing. New situations may be anticipated and misconstrued as recurrent trauma. The clarification of confusion, the undoing of denial, and distortion of reality, and of tendencies toward splitting of the ego and the object world, will require reconstruction of the traumatic situation with its external and internal coordinates.

The patient's past traumatic experience cannot be understood in depth in a here-and-now treatment which dispenses with genetic interpretation and reconstruction. Disguised derivatives of trauma in symptoms, transference, screen memories, nightmares, and so on, have to be analyzed to their genetic roots. A one-sided here-and-now or transference-only position may unwittingly become a shared denial of prior trauma and a turning away from recognition of the childish character of neurosis and its transference repetition. While the confusion of trauma and fantasy and single shock trauma models contributed to a technical shift away from reconstruction, the reconstruction and working through of trauma remains important within clinical analysis. The nature of "facts" and their meaning are interdependent and cannot be ascertained solely from external impressions, that is, manifest content. Psychoanalysis, as Brenner (1968) and others have emphasized, is a science. There is an art to our science, but psychoanalysis is a rational theory and therapy. We depend not only upon empathy and introspection but upon logic and coherence, an explanation which is parsimoniously comprehensive. The events of an individual's life, and in this case traumatic experience, cannot be fully appreciated or understood in isolation, but it seems impossible to assign meaning without the experience. Analytic interpretation is incomplete without the interplay and imbrication of reality and fantasy. Contrary to the notion of "narrative truth" (Spence, 1982), I would emphasize that there are actual experiences (with highly subjective meaning) which are part of the patient's authentic feeling about his own unique life and which lend rational conviction to the analytic autobiography. The accumulation of converging analytic evidence (e.g., about the need to justify one's having survived a sibling) to provoke punishment, and do penance for death wishes that become a reality, in which the parents were also traumatized and depressed, clarifies both cause and effect and the intrapsychic meaning and consequences of the loss.

The analytic autobiography is jointly revised and corrected and partially recreated by analyst and patient, but there are limits to how much is really created without doing violence to reality considerations and what Freud called historical truth. We have to be careful that the art of analysis does not subvert the science, and that we do not replace the patient's personal myth with analytic myth. In this connection, Freud's case histories are a unique blend of science and literature. The analytic exposition has permitted historical reconstruction so that virtually all of Freud's patients and other characters in the case histories have been identified.

The unconscious meaning and significance of trauma are also major facets of another problem, the relationship between trauma and neurosis. This problem has intrigued analysts, since a quantitative factor has always been implicated in the ego's failure to master danger and the ensuing neurotic compromise formations. In actual fact, a pure traumatic neurosis which did not involve internal conflicts remains a remote theoretical abstraction rather than a clinical entity. Beginning with representational thought and persisting fantasy, all individuals have both active and dormant conflicts which may be reinforced and reactivated in the traumatic situation. What we regularly find, then, is an admixture of trauma and neurosis in which neurotic dispositions and the accumulation of strain serve as predisposition and vulnerability to the consequences of the trauma and to further neurotic complications. Fantasies may be intensified, and then modified by traumatic experience. Unconscious fantasy is a preexisting determinant of the meaning of trauma, and the trauma is elaborated in an altered fantasy system. Fixations to trauma as well as fixations resulting from trauma are associated with a tendency toward regression (e.g., from oedipal conflict in cases of repeated childhood enemas). It is noteworthy that Freud (1939) described "traumas" in the development of a neurosis. Fenichel (1945) stated, "The distinction between traumatic neuroses and psychoneuroses is an artificial one. . . . There is no traumatic neurosis without psychoneurotic complications" (p. 541). Defense was activated by anxiety, and the motive for defense was the avoidance of automatic anxiety and trauma. While internal forces alone may prove to be traumatic, actual experience may be crucial in determining the nature of the trauma and the resources available for recovery.

The traumatized child's reactions have been influenced by the response of the involved objects. The child may provoke more of a response than anticipated, a different response than expected, and may be confronted with a very different outcome than originally envisioned. The actual experience will be invested with the child's preexisting fantasies so that a physical assault or a surgical procedure may be experienced as a castration threat or a punishment or a masochistic gratification, and so on. The

preexisting fantasies will appear to be validated and reinforced, and the younger the child the greater will be the
likelihood of confusion between fantasy and reality. The
fantasy may meet only a token or a highly intensified form
of validation so that there will be a variable codetermina-
tion of internal and external factors. While Freud and the
pioneers struggled with the difference between fantasy
and actual traumatic experience (e.g., in the case of the
primal scene), contemporary analysis assigns importance
to both the fantasy and the traumatic experience and dif-
ferentiates internal fantasy from actual trauma. The latter
may confirm the child's omnipotent expectations, while a
fantasy is much more under ego control and modulation
and subject to the individual's usual functioning defenses.
It is not the fantasy, then, but the realization or validation
of the fantasy in the form of traumatic experience that
contributes to traumatic fixation and vulnerability to repeated trauma (Greenacre, 1967). These interrelationships between unconscious fantasy, conflict, and trauma
may be in the contemporary foreground in those patients
traumatized by the acting out, illness, or death of their
therapist; iatrogenic trauma has its own problems for subsequent treatment and reconstruction.

Vulnerability to trauma is of two related types: vulnerability to the activation of neurotic conflict and unconscious fantasy, and vulnerability to the reactivation of
trauma. An old trauma may be repressed but may nevertheless result in a fresh traumatic state in the form of the
return of the repressed. No trauma is ever fully mastered
so that it cannot be reactivated given the appropriate internal–external releasing forces. One specific aspect of the
enduring change or ego alteration that is a consequence
of trauma is an expectable susceptibility to reactivation
of the trauma. Another aspect concerns generalized ego
weakness, and ego constriction may result from denial,
repression, or other traumatic aftereffects. Ego fragility

and rigidity may then predispose to fixation to trauma and a predisposition to regression and to neurosis. There is also susceptibility, it seems, not only to reactivation of the particular traumatic experience but reactivation of any and all trauma and associated unconscious conflict.

One traumatic experience may serve as a screen representation for others, and traumas may have cumulative and reciprocal influence (Khan, 1963). The case of a child of 4 years of age who witnessed the murder of her mother by her father, who then attempted suicide, was described by Bergen (1958). This girl was massively, multiply traumatized, suddenly and violently losing both parents. The many unconscious intrapsychic meanings of the traumas were analytically inferred (e.g., blaming herself for demanding mother's affection and eliciting rejection, an oedipal victory, castration and mutilation, and so on). However, the attribution to her mother's dying words warning the child away, as being especially traumatic, appears to be highly questionable in retrospect. In the face of the traumatic shocks and remobilized cumulative trauma, the remembered words may be appraised as a screen memory or screen trauma. This case vividly demonstrates the value of child analysis and reconstruction soon after the massive traumatic experience. The child's fantasies, conflicts, and constructs concerning the traumas were worked through with growth of her reality ego (Abrams, 1984).

Castration fears which have been associated with childhood tonsillectomy may also reactivate preoedipal anxieties of loss of body parts and contents, with regressive instability of the body image. The accumulation of multiple traumas is a function of both internal vulnerability and noxious experience, and may have determinants in unusual innate sensitivities (Bergman and Escalona, 1949) or parental dysfunction. (One is reminded again of Freud's "complemental series" [1916–1917, p. 362].) The structural consequences of trauma may be quite localized and discrete or widespread and diffuse. With some borderline or psychotic individuals, part of the structural deficit may represent both a predisposition to trauma and damage resulting from trauma in a deleterious, circular process. Trauma also has economic, dynamic, and genetic dimensions and can be understood within a metapsychological framework (Rangell, 1967).

Freud was not always consistent in his earlier and later views concerning the pathogenic effects of trauma. His 1937 formulation, that those neuroses which have a powerful traumatic element have the best prognosis, is highly controversial and not borne out by current clinical experience. Massively traumatized individuals are not easily treated and are sometimes inaccessible to psychoanalysis. Basic trust may be eroded; a sense of security and safety may be superseded by hypervigilance, searching for omens and premonitory warnings, or taking risks as though magically invulnerable. A permanent structural fragility or vulnerability to regression and reactivation of the trauma may ensue. The tendency to automatic rather than signal anxiety, the threat of revival of trauma in the treatment situation, the impairment of ego regulation and object relations may make for a most difficult treatment. Analytic experience indicates that such massive trauma need not have occurred in childhood to have severely damaging effects. Such trauma during adolescence or adult life, as, for example, occurred with victims of the Holocaust, indicates that there is probably a "breaking point" for all individuals and that recovery is a slow and usually incomplete process.

The importance of the personality prior to the massive trauma remains significant for recovery, but with great individual variation. Unconscious fantasy distortion and elaboration of protracted trauma condenses preexisting fantasy with subsequent fantasy overlay. Careful, patient reconstruction will be required to dissect the traumatic experience, and the associated affects and intrapsychic conflicts embedded in the unconscious fantasy constellation. One trauma may be a defense against others, or represent a cumulative traumatic experience, or serve as a metaphor for the patient's initial narrative construction. What is now more important than the recovery of repressed memories, is the conscious and unconscious meaning of the traumatic experience, and the systematic analysis and working through of the traumatic sequellae, and concurrent unconscious conflicts. Psychosomatic reactions are universal. The tortured person continues to be internally tormented. In addition to an altered or shattered sense of self, the external world of the massively traumatized survivor may also have been shattered, with its own intrapsychic reverberations. The self and object world will never be the same, and certain values, ideals, and expectations may be radically changed. The inevitable conscious questions of why, why me, and why not another, defy rational explanation, but are significantly linked to the survivor's unconscious fantasies. As analysis oscillates between the present and the traumatic past, the analytic attitude and countertransference will be of crucial import to the process of reconstruction.

Fixation to trauma is variously indicated, for example, by avoidance, numbing, and altered states of consciousness; by intrusive repetition into thoughts, feelings, and behavior. There may be relative amnesia, affectless memory, or traumatic memories with fantasy distortions. The traumatic play of children tends to be driven, and less voluntary, flexible, and pleasurable. While traumatic repetitions and the provocation of possible further trauma may be active attempts to regulate, integrate, and master trauma, they may also convert acute traumatic situations to a chronic traumatic neurosis. The patient may be silent, unaware, or unable to confront or discuss the chronic traumatic experience. Some traumatized patients avoid any conscious reference to trauma, and others are overtly preoccupied with "the trauma" and talk about it incessantly.

The pathogenic effects of trauma may be minimal or devastating. Probably, only uncommonly resourceful patients (e.g., artists and analysts) can make beneficial use of such adversity. Some survivors of massive trauma have "amazingly" reconstituted, gaining new skills and sublimations. Some "invulnerables" seem to negotiate severe childhood traumas with surprising strength and only mild disturbance—at least so it seems pending further research. This brings us to the question of whether trauma can be constructive and whether trauma serves not only as a sensitizing experience, leaving areas of susceptibility, but also as an immunizing and strengthening experience. If we adhere to the narrower definition of trauma in the sense of the shattering experience which overwhelms the ego and results in helplessness and panic (automatic anxiety), then the aftereffect cannot be simply beneficial or likely to result in immunization. It is possible that as a result of the assimilation and repair, mourning and new adaptation, resourceful individuals may be better prepared to deal with particular aspects of shock or assault. Preparation, rather than being taken by surprise, and the capacity of the ego to adapt, are important ego functions, but they do not undo the pathogenic effects of traumas.

While the individual may be strengthened in some areas, vulnerability and structural alteration occur in other areas, and it does not seem particularly wise to conclude that traumatic damage is outweighed by the benefits. A constructive recovery might be more likely given further benevolent development with favorable object relationships and identifications. For example, the recovery of a traumatized child will be aided if the parents were not simultaneously traumatized and are emotionally available to the child. On the other hand, parents who contribute to the child's trauma may be regarded as a continuing threat, may not be able to comfort or console, and may undermine rather than promote recovery and ego mastery. Identification with the aggressor (and with aggressive affects and behaviors), and with other familial victims, intensifies sadomasochistic patterns as well as the sadistic and punitive dimensions of the superego. The identifications which follow traumatic experience serve defense and mastery as well as the vicarious gratification of forbidden impulses.

Greenacre (1967) noted that an in-phase or phase-specific trauma such as a castration threat during oedipal development may reinforce the dominant phase or may regressively reinstate an earlier phase. Out-of-phase traumas may lead to peculiar patterns of gratification and phase disorganization. If the ego is really incapacitated, trauma cannot be expected to elicit a developmentally appropriate response. In the case of children who have experienced assault (e.g., in the form of beatings or immobilized bondage, or children who have been sexually molested), the earlier emphasis on the inability of the child to achieve discharge of pent-up tension has given way to a more comprehensive understanding of the influence of the child's overall development. Structural damage may result from the trauma, but also from recurrent traumatic anxiety, the pathogenic effects of excessive repression and denial, feelings of guilt and self-imposed punishment, and the influence of the repetition compulsion or tendencies toward serious acting out. Early traumatization may lead to delinquent destructiveness or to self-destructive tendencies. In the course of turning passive into active, some individuals repeat and inflict the trauma on other helpless individuals, an element in the abused children who become abusive parents. The majority of rapists have a history of sexual and aggressive abuse in their own childhood, and the aggression against the child inherent in the sexual seduction of the child should not be overlooked. In many instances parental (incestuous) sexual stimulation of the child has also been associated with punitive violence. Many sexually abused children have been genitally mutilated; if this has not been traumatic to the caretakers, and this is a significant question, it has been shocking to many caseworkers. Even where the children (and adults) claim to enjoy or benefit from the incestuous contact, initial shock effects may be covered by strain patterns, secondary gain, and defensive collusion with the abusive caretaker.

The child is often abjectly dependent on the abusive parent. The passive parent who colludes and condones fails to protect the child, fails to serve as an auxiliary ego for the child and superego for the spouse. In father–daughter incest, the mother may be a silent partner, but she will be blamed by the daughter for lack of protection and for vicarious participation. Fantasies of rescue and splitting of the parent image into protective and persecutory representations are common. Incest may defend against as well as express aggression; it may appear as the lesser evil in comparison to object loss or neglect. Some children prefer to be beaten rather than neglected (Berliner, 1947; Glenn, 1984). The organizing effect may be different, dependent on the conditions and content of the abuse; for example, whether the abuse is primarily sexual or aggressive. All traumas may be secondarily erotized for defensive and adaptive purposes, and because of regressive reinstinctualization of ego functions. The frequency, intensity, duration, and nature of the trauma, the reactions and responses of the parents and other caregivers, are all-important in the organizing influence of the trauma on the personality and subsequent development. The abused child has often lived in a punitive atmosphere, and may experience cumulative trauma, scapegoating, and inconsistent care. Such traumatized children tend to be hypervigilant and distrustful, with impaired narcissism, object relations, ego, and superego development. Relationships, activities, and interests may remain highly ambivalent, shallow, and lacking in sublimation. Much depends on the child's capacity to elicit, and the abusive parents' capacity to offer, some love, protection, and assistance. The defensive and adaptive love of a brutal "Big Brother" (Orwell's *1984*) should not obscure the question of Big Brother's love both within the abuse and alternating with it.

Psychological trauma is often reciprocally interwoven with physical trauma as in severe illness, injury (frequently to the head and genitals in child abuse), malnutrition (as in the survivor syndrome), and so on. The reconstruction of multiple traumas and severe strain over extended periods of time, and different developmental phases, is a formidable task. Reconstruction of trauma is an integrative act which connects past and present, cause and effect on new levels of developmental organization, restoring personality continuity. Reconstruction involves the internal structures and fantasies, the influence of the child's object world on the child, the child's influence on the caretakers, and the particular personality organization and developmental phase at the time of the trauma, and as the personality is altered afterwards, by the trauma.

In those instances where the trauma has been successfully repressed and isolated from the rest of the personality we may see gaps in memory, conspicuous silences, isolated dreams without associations, dreams within dreams, or hallucinatory and delusional breaks with reality in the presence of otherwise sound reality testing (Greenacre, 1956). I believe that these are the less common and more atypical forms in which we encounter repressed traumatic experience in psychoanalysis. The concomitant use of denial and isolation, the need to continue denial in extended situations in adult life, the significance of denial in fantasy, words, and deeds, all point to a past traumatic reality which is being disavowed. I have given a particular example of such a use of denial (Blum, 1983) in a patient who began his analysis with a lie that his mother had died, a lie which served and continued denial on many levels. The lie denied his mother's current illness, the trauma of his father's death, and a still earlier repressed trauma of his mother's attempted suicide, with the associated possible homicidal annihilation of the entire family. The lie then also referred to the familial fabrications which covered over the mother's having turned on the gas in a self-destructive and destructive act from which the family nevertheless survived physically intact. In this sense, the very important traumatic experience of the father's death was simultaneously a screen memory which condensed early and later traumas and which served defensive functions. The lie about death meant death was a lie, that all loss could be restored, all injuries repaired. The lie of the parent's death undid the death, bartered the life of one parent for the other, and in the transference was an act of derisive aggression against both the deserting and surviving parent. By breaking off the analysis with the lie and then resuming the analysis, the patient symbolically enacted the killing and resurrection of the analyst-parent and continued to deny the irreversibility of death. The trauma was thus repeated in the transference from the outset of treatment and repeated time and again in dreams, symptoms, fantasies, and associations throughout the treatment and especially at termination. Reconstruction resolved where the truth lay, and helped uncover the historic truth within the patient's fabrication and fantasies. Identifying with the unwavering search for the truth in the analytic process, the patient could understand present anticipation and provocation of loss in relation to parent loss in childhood, and unconscious conflict over his own and his parents' aggression.

Nightmares and night terrors are gross indications of trauma. But more subtle indications of trauma appear in fantasy play, repetitive daydreams and dreams, screen memories, peculiar ego states or dystonic moods, and disguised partial often unnoticed reenactments which may be well rationalized and often seemed adaptive to reality. A patient who wanted to open a window because the office was stuffy had survived smoke asphyxiation which killed others in the family. Trauma may be a major determinant of acting out in analysis and in life, as in some patients with repetitive accidents, masochistic rituals, and perversions.

The occurrence of multiple traumas and the presence of strain, such as chronic seductiveness or chronic depression of the surviving parent prior to and after parent loss, greatly complicates the task of reconstruction. Patterns of object relationship and identification may be reconstructed in conjunction with serial traumatic events, contributing to analytic revision of self and object representations. A mother's resort to forced feeding, enemas, and laxatives, and threatening stories indicate a pattern of coercion which is essential to reconstruction. The strain patterns and condensation of traumas are also related to the phenomenon of the telescoping of trauma (A. Freud, 1951) so that what seems like one overwhelming experience may actually have been repeated many times and may represent the condensation of other injuries, disappointments, and frustrations as well. The telescoping effect results from condensation, but also from ego defense and synthesis. A traumatic or nodal "event" is in itself overdetermined and complex, of necessity rather isolated from the totality of experience in the process of reconstruction.

Trauma, as Kris (1956a) observed, tends to fuse with its aftermath. Also, the child inevitably tends to confuse trauma with punishment. Destiny has been malevolent so that the parent, usually the mother (lady luck), is blamed.

The mother is usually blamed for her own or her child's severe illness, and may be irrationally regarded as an abusive villain by the child "victim," who may reciprocally try to victimize and villify the mother or her representatives. In the child's magical world, there is omnipotent protection and omnipotent punishment. The traumatized child is often convinced of his own badness, with heightened tendencies toward guilt, self-reproach, and low self-esteem. The child identifies with the aggressor and transgressor but also with the parent's defenses and guilt, and other affects. The child may identify with the parent's self-blame, and with the parent's feeling punished through the child's trauma. In some situations the child and parent have shared fantasies about the trauma and its elaboration.

There are affective responses and communications which are often derailed in the traumatic situation and its aftermath. The range, quality, and intensity of affect expression may be altered by trauma. I have referred to the aggression against the child which may be disguised in playful seduction and rationalizations of physical expressions of love. In my experience, trauma has always been associated not only with automatic anxiety but with enormous anger, with rage. The traumatized child may fear his own rage and the rage of the parent or authorities. He may not be able to recognize, express, or assimilate his own rage. The child's cries, complaints, and protests may have been stifled. In any case, the traumatic situation does not permit reflection or verbalization. If the analyst fails to recognize the cry for help, the silent scream, the strangulated terror and rage, then he or she may join in a shared defense. Reconstruction (within the analytic process as a whole) reintegrates dissociated and altered ego states with cognitive and affective working through of the traumatic experience.

We are only able to approximate for the patient the nature of traumatic experience as well as its most important internal meaning and consequences. However, the patient's life history, past and present, the nature of the psychopathology, and the unfolding of the transference will all provide evidence for an educated analytic inference of real trauma. Freud (1926b) referred to the sometimes "irrefutable evidence that these occurrences which we had inferred really did take place" and he then asserted: "The correct reconstruction, you must know, of such forgotten experiences of childhood always has a great therapeutic effect, whether they permit of objective confirmation or not. These events owe their importance, of course, to their having occurred at such an early age, at a time when they could still produce a traumatic effect on the feeble ego" (p. 216).

The importance of the patient's preexisting personality and the vulnerability of ego immaturity may have to be qualified in the case of massive trauma such as that resulting from the Holocaust (Niederland, 1968; Bergmann and Jucovy, 1982). The massive protracted traumatization often has had similar effects, regardless of the preexisting personality and mature age of the patient. It is, however, impossible to generalize, since we are dealing with a heterogeneous group which has suffered various forms of trauma and has had different posttraumatic experiences which could promote or retard recovery. There is no consensual definition of a survivor; one case may be more concerned with guilt, arrested mourning, and fear of further loss; another with repetitive reenactment of trauma associated with fantasies of sacrifice, salvation, and resurrection. Those patients who successfully resurrected and reconstituted their lives were far less likely to become analytic patients. Some such patients (but not all) show similar symptoms (e.g., depression and nightmares) and impaired ego functioning with perhaps irreversible damage to psychic structure. Massive extended trauma differs from the usual concept of trauma which is that of an incapacitating ego shock in a short period of time. The massive traumas of adult life may be comparable in their global effect in breaking down already formed structure, to trauma in the infant which leads to damage or arrest in the formation of structure. The greater the vulnerability and the more massive the trauma, the more profound and pervasive are the structural impairments. Developmentally, vulnerability is greater during preoedipal structural differentiation than during postoedipal structural consolidation.

Prior to ego differentiation, the concept of psychic trauma may not be applicable, and it would be more appropriate to think of organismic trauma and distress. There are special difficulties attached to preverbal reconstruction of such traumatic experience. The residues of such traumatic experience may only appear in sensory, motor, and psychosomatic phenomena in sensations, feelings, and images. Certain important developmental acquisitions such as signal anxiety, basic trust, self and object constancy, or their failures may aid in reconstruction, but do not readily distinguish between trauma, constitutional deficits in structure formation, environmental failure, and developmental malformation. The earlier the reconstruction in terms of developmental level, the greater reliance on imagination and speculation. It must also be borne in mind that the differential regression seen in psychosis and other serious disorders does not recapitulate developmental differentiation and sequence. Regression from more advanced phases distorts the original picture, just as the earlier phases are transformed in later developmental reorganization and later verbalized in the course of conceptualization. Suffice it to say, the data from psychotics, borderlines, and direct child observation supplement analytic data, but many questions remain regarding inferences, hypotheses, and reconstructions of the preverbal period. At the same time, our increasing knowledge of early development, and our articulation and integration of analytic and developmental data, have advanced the accuracy and depth of reconstruction and hold promise as major areas of ongoing analytic research.

All the examples, so far, have clearly represented overstimulation. But what about those individuals traumatized in states of understimulation, in physical and emotional isolation with lack of stimulus nutriments? In early infancy, we are reminded of maternal deprivation syndromes. In adult life lack of stimulus nutriment undermines ego autonomy from the drives. In the case of stimulus deprivation, the organism is flooded by internal tension, by lack of opportunity for appropriate discharge, and by unbearable frustrations, and so on. I would emphasize the helplessness of the ego in the face of either deprivation and overstimulation. The emphasis in the early literature on overstimulation does not do justice to more contemporary concerns, not only with quantity but with quality and consistency of experience, particularly as it refers to what is developmentally appropriate. Anomalous forms of stimulation and experience may result in strain or actual trauma.

Living conditions, parental relationships, social class, cultural bias, family size, and child-rearing practices all influence development and predispose to certain types of trauma. Rampant divorce may be associated with parent loss and inconsistent parenting; overcrowding with exposure to the primal scene, birth, and death; social persecution will be linked to unconscious narcissistic and castration trauma. Perhaps protracted incestuous relationships take on new meanings and special adaptations. Where there is cultural condoning (in degree) of primal scene exposure and incestuous seduction, superficial ego-syntonic acceptance of such behavior may be more likely, with massive resistance to recognition of the pathogenic influence of overstimulation and strain.

It is probable that cultural condoning of a particular trauma may reduce the traumatic impact, in certain respects, and that it may prepare the growing child for experiences that would otherwise be more traumatic for that individual. At the same time, there are universals in the human condition. The innocence of childhood and the conflict-free utopian rearing of children in primitive societies are myths which deny the traumas of childhood and the highly conflicted and too often tragic aspects of human existence. The ubiquity of unconscious conflict and childhood traumas in all cultures cautions against developmental inferences based on external impressions and manifest content.

Chapter Four

Neurotic and Physical Illness: A Specific Reconstruction in the Analytic Process

This unusual and fascinating case demonstrated the technique and effects of reconstruction, with a specific, circumscribed reconstruction in an analytic process. The reconstruction was adventitiously suited to the heuristic purposes of the research. As an analytic intervention, the reconstruction particularly utilized the transference, the totality of the analytic data, and the patient's life history; it explained current phenomenology and, at the same time, connected past and present in a form which was mutually clarifying and enlarged analytic explanation. This was contrasted with other cases where the analyst's private construction either did not become reconstruction to be shared with the patient or where the linking of past and present, the interplay of internal and external factors, fantasy and reality, could not be demonstrated. While the analyst regretted the fact that the reconstruction was not complete and that it was perhaps too narrowly based upon prototypical issues of childhood trauma, it was nevertheless theoretically and therapeutically useful. Because of circumstances not then known, however, the reconstruction was powerless to alter one of the patient's primary complaints, although clearly efficacious in other areas. Simply stated, this was a reconstruction of the effects of circumcision at age 5 as a phase-specific oedipal trauma. This reconstruction led in ever-widening scope and depth to a consideration of the patient's antecedent problems and their reorganization in relation to important experiences in later life.

A prime consideration was the fact that an anti-Semitic transference neurosis was developing with all its overdetermined meanings. The content was dominated by fantasies about the analyst as a Jew. The anti-Semitic transference responded to the reconstruction within the analytic process, despite the fact that the anti-Semitism was not explicitly implicated in the reconstruction. Furthermore, a current, castrating, unrecognized, organic trauma was, in all probability, under way during the course of the analysis. The psychological dimensions of the patient's problems yielded to reconstruction and the further progress of the analysis, but the symptoms, due to organic causes, did not remit. Ultimately, it was the failure of the analysis to ameliorate the patient's physical symptoms of pains and abnormal sensations which contributed to the patient finally discontinuing the analytic treatment. When the diagnosis was made, there was already quite significant analytic progress and improvement.

At the time of the analysis, neither analyst nor patient was consciously aware of the progressive organic penile (Peyronie's) disease with which the patient was afflicted. Retrospectively, the analyst perspicaciously considered that an independent test of the validity and therapeutic effect of reconstruction had occurred. The positive effect of the reconstruction upon the analytic process and progress could not be credited to suggestion, transference cure, or the utilization of inexact, incomplete reconstruction for defensive purposes.

There were many differences of opinion in the group concerning the timing and readiness for reconstruction, the inventiveness and ingenuity of the analyst versus the patient's capacity for self-discovery and joint shaping of the reconstruction, and the impact of the reconstruction in the face of such a severe emerging organic illness which added an observable reality to childhood anxieties about his penis. The single event no longer had the significance of a single shock trauma, as in the pioneer days of psychoanalysis, but it could be seen to be related to a variety of developmental, genetic, and dynamic issues. From the beginning, the analyst and the group were interested in exploring the patient's developmental phases, their interrelationship, and the patient's drive and personality organization at different points in his life and certain patterns in the patient's life such as his tendency toward compliance, lack of assertiveness, and inhibition of aggression with inability to recognize and express his inner rage. The overwhelming nature of his conflicts and anxieties coexisted with sufficient ego strength and resources for the patient to be able to participate and benefit from an analytic process. The patient was analyzed under extraordinary life circumstances and unforeseen current strains and traumatic experience. Despite the fact that the case was not a completed analysis, it was a remarkable learning experience and richly rewarded the research group by the stimulating questions and insights that were derived from the presentation. The analysis was conducted with standard procedure, four times a week.

The material was chosen primarily from the period of the first forty-two months of analysis. The basis for presentation was reasonably detailed notes dictated immediately after each hour. Dr. A chose the material upon the basis of what was most interesting to him in terms of the clinical problems and the research aims and efforts which might then be illuminated from multiple perspectives. Discussion was spontaneous after the presentation of the analytic data, with members of the group commenting on the case, the analytic work and style, the sources and nature of the reconstruction, and the impact of the reconstruction on the analytic process. The fresh and fascinating clinical material also evoked clinical vignettes of related analytic experiences by the members of the group, theoretical and technical excursions, and numerous analytic exchanges with each other concerning both shared and different points of view. There were continuing attempts to define the nature and process of reconstruction and to share different views so that clarifications could be achieved and problems and perplexities highlighted. For example, when reconstructions as specific technical interventions are differentiated both from genetic interpretations and from the larger analytic process as a whole, there are other issues that might seem even more puzzling than in the initial review of reconstruction. The latter could be seen as more remote from the immediacy of the here-and-now of the transference, yet more enlightening for the analyst than transference reactions or memories alone. The reconstruction both derived from and ordered the analytic data so that the transference could be understood as a repetition. It was a repetition, in this case, that was intimately linked to the activating, shaping, and adaptive needs of a threatening current illness. The patient was afraid of losing his penis, his motility, and his mother—self and object loss associated with regressive loss of a stable mature psychic organization.

From the outset, it was clear that the knowledge of the patient's organic illness would have influenced the understanding of the analytic data and research issues and hypotheses. This was balanced by consistent attempts at interpretation of tendencies toward "retrospective falsification," so that the differences between a prospective and retrospective view of the issues are brought into open analytic discourse.

The patient was a young, married, male adult who first developed symptoms after a brief affair during a work assignment while separated from his wife. He had confessed this indiscretion to his wife who had picked up on the fact of his continuing attachment to the other woman. In fact, he was ambivalent about returning to his wife and continued to be preoccupied with his lover. He had contracted gonorrhea from her, and alternated between visions of her as promiscuous or as an innocent, duped by an unscrupulous exfiancé. He was quite anxious.

He also complained of aching in both legs, present for about a dozen years. Repeated consultations and examinations had all concluded that the pain was of psychological origin. It should also be stated that early in the analysis he began to mention, occasionally, some aching pain in his penis with extended prolongation of erection. He developed severe apprehension and preoccupation with his condition. The case was further complicated by three additional, important issues during the first eighteen months of analytic work. The patient's mother developed cancer and died; the analyst was then out with a threatening illness for three months; and the patient's father-in-law died, which led to new stresses and alterations in his life situation. This particular sequence of traumas had a major impact upon the analysis. The current situation in some ways powerfully activated earlier conflicts and traumas, bringing them more into analytic focus while at the same time tending to obscure the past in the crises and emergencies of the present. It became important to reconstruct the present to understand how and why the patient fell ill and the effect of the current crises upon the patient. It was equally important to understand the complex relationship between the present and the past in which the influence of the past was sometimes dimly apprehended through a glass darkly, and was sometimes intrusive, in overshadowing the patient's current life.

The patient soon began carefully to monitor his pains as related to the vicissitudes of analysis. They were worse or better over the weekend; worse or better when he was seeing the analyst, and the aching in his penis became laden with transference implications. Until the time of the reconstruction, there was growing anti-Semitic feeling. In fact, he had little preadult contact with Jews and, prior to analysis, such issues had no conscious importance to him. The patient talked about Jews in general, and such things as the analyst being or not being Jewish; Jewish blackmail, exploitation, and greed; financial avarice; Jews taking his and other people's money. A defensive style soon became apparent in which thoughts were used to "push away other thoughts." He "complied" with the fundamental rule by producing a profusion of dreams, memories, and fantasy material with a markedly phallic cast. He dreamed of trying to escape and running into a woman's bathroom. He had the feeling, while telling the dream, as if he was pursued by a man; he then thought about hearing a woman urinating in the woman's bathroom in the setting of the analytic office. This led to his frequent urination and going to the bathroom before every analytic hour. He was afraid of intruders in the bathroom when he was urinating or having a bowel movement, afraid of his mother or grandmother knowing that he masturbated. His mother was going to have surgery at the time when a fatal malignancy was discovered.

The patient came from a rural background. He was particularly involved with two brothers, one two years younger and another born when he was at puberty. He envied these two siblings because of their freewheeling aggressiveness and devil-may-care attitudes but frowned on the anxiety they caused his mother. The youngest brother was born with a crippling congenital deformity affecting his legs. This compounded the earlier trauma of the birth of his other brother. The birth of this physically handicapped child was a severe stress for the entire family and doubtless contributed to the patient's adolescent difficulties. After the birth of the deformed sibling, he remembered dressing up in his mother's clothes. This included putting on her bra with some rags in the bra. He pretended he was a woman while he denied wanting to be a woman. He wanted to know what it felt like to be a woman and thought of putting his penis and testes between his legs so that he would look like a woman. As a woman he would be able to have multiple orgasms. As a college student he would walk about in a closed raincoat, concealing the erection protruding through his fly.

In the very next hour, he reported that the doctor had informed his father that his mother had only several months to live. He felt he had to hold back his feelings—it would not be manly to be upset, and he did not want to cry in front of the analyst or his wife. Typically, the patient again returned to his gender and body preoccupations. In grammar school he believed that girls urinated through the back, but perhaps he also had this thought during college. He would masturbate with rubberbands around his genitals. This adult practice would prolong erection and reassure him about potency and penis size. At one time he masturbated with a plastic bag which broke so that he ejaculated semen onto his face. Turning back to the subject of his mother and his inability to cry, he was serious with God while fearful of the wrath of Heaven. Watches needed repair as his mother's time was running out and pieces were broken off furniture. Interchanged with images of his mother ill in bed were pictures of her having intercourse. A woman could be hurt during intercourse, and this would be the source of physical disability. She would not be able to walk normally (like his crippled brother and his fears about himself). More and more the penis preoccupations, his feminine and masculine wishes, his symptoms, and his mother's illness came to the fore in connection with the rising preoccupation with the analyst's Jewishness. The transference was deepening as his mother was dying. Some of his symptoms were only much later revealed to be of organic origin.

The patient not only had fantasies of himself exposed with his fly open and in the nude; he also took photographs of his genitals and thought of a poster of a black native with his penis tied in a knot. The black male's penis was probably related to the issue of anti-Semitic blackmail, but also to curiosity concerning the size of penises and what happened with erection. The patient felt he had a small penis which reassuringly enlarged with erection. Contrary to the usual childhood fantasy, he imagined his penis as larger than his father's very small penis. He recalled school scenes of boys who threatened to cut the penis off another boy; kids chasing a boy and shouting that he would be caught and have his penis cut off. Sadomasochistic primal scene material appeared when he thought of a movie where a girl watched her mother make love, and then the girl killed one of the lovers. Proposing that Jewish doctors were able to influence women to pleasurable arousal, for the first time the patient reported his wife's name. He was threatened by enormous castration anxiety and worried that he would only be able to gratify a woman with his fingers. Actually, losing his mother, he could not confront the fear of losing his wife. He was increasingly unnerved by her many demands—for affection, money, and a baby.

The technical dilemma for the analyst concerned what to interpret for himself and his own understanding of the transference. Clarifying what seemed so mysterious, difficult, and intensely conflict-laden involved unraveling the confluence of different latent material with manifestly phallic preoccupation. The bodily concerns were also apparently related to the body itself as a phallus as well as to a castrated body image, the deformed brother, and the surgically wounded dying mother. He both hid his penis to protect himself from castration and, at the same time, displayed his penis to reassure himself of its presence and his phallic strength. In that way his potency and power were not lost, and he was not a loser. His penisless father was identified not only with the mother but also with the congenitally crippled brother. The massive denial and the magical nature of his identifications stimulated much discussion of early developmental issues versus the current threatened losses. The massive denial also may have reactivated earlier denial in fantasy and, concretely, in enactment. Confusion and disorganization were related to current concerns about his penis and object loss, but also to unresolved conflicts from early life. He was so overwhelmed that he was afraid of going crazy and of driving the analyst crazy. When the analyst became ill, the patient became extremely fearful of his own aggression and its terrible consequences. His seemingly phallic sexualization defended against aggression and the fantasies and realities of bodily damage. All the patient's disorganizing anxieties were channeled into the central preoccupation with his penis. He was like a little boy who touched his penis for reassurance whenever he was anxious. The patient would psychologically touch this area in repetitive fantasies of concealing, stealing, enlarging, and shrinking the penis, and, in games of let's pretend, he was a woman with and without a penis. He retained the omnipotentiality of being both male and female, father and mother. He attempted to deny the terrible tragedy of a family where his mother was dying and children had serious organic conditions.

Consideration of Theoretical Issues: Identifications and Developmental Phase Considerations

The analyst had learned, early in the analysis, that there had been an operation on the patient's penis which the analyst deduced was a circumcision. Wondering about cause and effect and developmental sequence, the analyst waited until he had enough grasp of the data to infer that the circumcision had been a central issue—an oedipal trauma which had organized antecedent and subsequent development. The analyst had been out with illness for six weeks when the patient focused upon the patient's operation. The transference which repeated the past was also activated by the current context of the analyst's illness, the patient's mother's illness, and the patient's relatively silent illness. The periodic aching in the patient's penis with sustained erection and the pains in his legs were reported as actually not as bad during the analyst's absence. As the patient thought of his bedridden mother, he shifted to anxieties about possibly having a daughter to whom he would be sexually attracted during her puberty. Returning to the problem of urinating publicly, he recalled an operation on his penis when he was 4 or 5 to alleviate his inability to urinate properly. Could he have a son?

There appeared to be a readiness for reconstruction on the part of the patient and the analyst. The specific reconstruction, which emerged from the analytic process, was that the patient had been traumatized by a circumcision during his fourth year for the treatment of a penile infection and phimosis. This reconstruction was related to the ego confusion, the disorganization, the anxieties on the oedipal level, as well as the prephallic regression and preoedipal problems. The analyst's illness had made the patient extraordinarily anxious, and he was now afraid of both seduction and his own aggression. In some respects, this was thought to recapitulate elements of the patient's oedipal phase and adolescence. The reconstruction was shaped by the present and the past and linked the present illnesses to the traumatic past. The reconstruction was broader than a genetic interpretation and integrated a number of memories and data from different developmental phases. The very notion of a phase-specific trauma was questioned and usually can be demonstrated to be an oversimplification. As the reconstruction was enlarged, it was also noted that the patient utilized massive denial and fantasy. Some analysts emphasized the continuation of denial and fetishistic tendencies from infancy and early childhood, while others emphasized the emergency use of massive denial with respect to current illnesses.

The reconstruction was also an integration of development on a higher level of organization than interpretation and served as a guiding principle for further analytic interpretation. The process of reconstruction was by no means identical with the analytic process itself. The genetic point of view and developmental considerations figured prominently in the process of reconstruction, and reconstruction, in turn, provided a guiding perspective for the understanding of transference repetition and pathogenesis. Reconstruction encompassed the patient's past and present illnesses, his childhood surgery, his mother's surgery, and the birth of the crippled brother early in the patient's adolescence. Having begun as a preliminary construction in the analyst's mind, the reconstruction itself was subjected to the patient's working through and further modification. The reconstruction itself was drawn into the transference and the analytic process.

Denial and possible subliminal awareness of his real, slowly progressive disease process led to further questions concerning the new emergence of loss versus the revival of past experiences of injury and loss. Had the mother also suffered from prodromal and progressive symptoms?

Was there denial on her part or on the part of the family of her malignancy? Had she delayed seeking medical advice and could the cancer have been arrested or cured if treated earlier? Similar questions applied to fantasies about the analyst's illness and his absence.

Given the patient's analytic and life history, was his fear of being a woman and his wish to be a woman a retreat from adolescent anxieties to anchorage in the oedipal phase or to an earlier developmental fixation or arrest? A partial, preoedipal developmental arrest may never have permitted the patient firmly to advance without continuous regressive tendencies and intermingling of phases. From the genetic point of view and appropriate genetic interpretation and reconstruction, it was important to understand whether the patient was both anxious and afraid to assume a phallic masculine position. The nature of his fluid, archaic, bisexual identifications, his magical and concrete thinking pointed to prephallic problems in which the anxieties of castration, loss of the object's love, and loss of the object were amalgamated.

The patient definitely defended against castration by saying, "I'm castrated already," since he could not be castrated with his penis hidden. He also hid his penis under feminine clothes as a phallic woman, denying both male and female castration. He was both man and woman. To enter the woman's bathroom was a symbolic representation of entering her genitals and pretending that he was a woman. But was this only a pubertal game?

Certainly similarities of this patient with the Wolf Man were observed. He fell ill after an attack of gonorrhea, developed phallic narcissistic preoccupations, and manifested powerful feminine identifications, especially with the mother in the primal scene. The current castration threat seemed to have induced a very severe regression in which identification with the fatally ill mother activated archaic anxieties and identifications. Something terrible was also happening to him which had to be denied. He also defended himself by magical identifications with concurrent projection in his anti-Semitism.

Assuming the role of a woman might not only protect against castration, but it could be related to the child's fantasy concerning the mother's feelings about the child. Identifications with the mother could also reassure the child through imagining how mother felt and empathically experienced the child, how much pleasure she derived from the child. Trial identifications would contribute to the affective experience, sexual relationships, Jewish relationships, and the marriage relationship.

Despite manifest oedipal conflicts, the primitive magical identifications and need for enactment in crossdressing were increasingly emphasized in discussion. The patient's florid fantasy life, concrete reenactments, and magical mirror types of identifications were present without the patient being fully aware of his penile illness. There was no sign, at that time, of actual penile deformity or an erectile disturbance. As in many cases with fetishistic and homosexual tendencies, the prephallic issues seemed to be increasingly paramount without neglecting the influence of later development. The birth of the patient's next younger brother was a narcissistic blow and maternal loss. The experience of the loss of the mother's availability at this time was presumed to be significantly related to the patient's primitive identifications with her during separation-individuation. Furthermore, his sibling's birth was associated with regression and enormous rage at the betraying mother and intruding sibling. Thus, in the process of reconstruction, the trauma of the circumcision reactivated the preoedipal trauma of sibling birth and was, in turn, reorganized by the strains of his adolescence and the patient's traumatizing current illness. Reconstruction took into account the constant interplay of reality and fantasy, external and internal factors, and the patient's own selection and synthesis. The clarity of the reconstruction contrasted with the patient's "Uh-huh" responses. The patient's affect was dampened, and the process of denial continued. From the point of view of the present threatening illness, the reconstruction offered a flight into the past and a continued avoidance of the terrifying realities of the present. Clarifying this interpenetration of reality and fantasy, the reconstruction was also clarified in relation to the transference. In addition to the organic disease process, the analytic processes also put stress upon the patient's thoroughly threatened phallic oedipal position. Interestingly enough, the patient's work was possibly dangerous but simultaneously offered a counterphobic defense. He suffered not only from reminiscences but also from premonitions of traumatic disaster. And the analyst was the strange Jewish man behind the couch who would take his pound of flesh, his mother, his money, and his penis—leaving the patient emasculated and helpless. The patient's perseveration about his penis pointed to the nature of the current illness and current illnesses in the analyst-father and his actual mother. Prephallic problems were inferred to have led to the unstable personality organization. His later development appeared to have been built on a shaky foundation.

The case presented many questions concerning the timing, form, and content of the reconstruction. How long does the analyst wait, and how much material and evidence are needed? The analyst responds to the totality of the analytic data, his knowledge of the patient's history and development, and his knowledge of normal development and psychopathology. The analyst makes continuous connections, selects trends, and analyzes the whole transference–countertransference interaction. In the early days of psychoanalysis when reconstruction was closely tied to traumatic events, there may have been early indications for reconstruction and a tendency to reconstruct, as Freud did very early in analysis. The early analyses themselves were usually very short by contemporary standards. Today, the complex fabric of developmental sequence and organization is a far more important context than the relatively simple timing of trauma. Temporal sequence has been replaced by developmental sequence and a greater appreciation of phase overlap and developmental transformation. The whole style and form of reconstruction gradually changed in the successive periods of analytic theoretical development and with the evolution of the theory of technique. Analysts also disengaged from their identification with Freud's and the pioneers' styles. Freud did not publish case histories after 1920 so that his own reconstructions were based upon the more limited theoretical outlook and experience of the pioneer years of analysis.

Changes in thinking about reconstruction and some of the controversies could be readily discerned in the discussion of the case. Emphasis upon the external reality factors, doubtless of great importance, were increasingly balanced with consideration, not only of the internal psychic reality of the patient, but also the entire development of the patient's disturbance. Memories were registered in terms of the patient's psychic reality, but the retrieved memories, as Freud had noted, were also colored by and connected to the patient's current life situation and adult personality organization.

In this case, the conviction of the treating analyst was equivalent to the conviction achieved by the patient. The patient was disappointed; the reconstruction, predictably, did not cure symptoms of organic origin. The case would never be carried to successful termination. How much conviction concerning the value and validity of the reconstruction was there among the research analysts?

There were certainly differences of opinion concerning the importance of the circumcision and its singular influence upon later development. The regressive, perverse behavior during adolescence was predominantly emphasized as indicative of powerful unresolved oedipal and preoedipal problems. The patient was overwhelmed by traumatic anxieties prior to the current illnesses, and there was evidence for a failure of a modulation of anxiety and other affects in the form of signals. What was questioned about the reconstruction was, therefore, not so much the validity of the specific reconstruction of circumcision but rather its overall importance and therapeutic benefit.

The questions of validity of the reconstruction also were linked to the issue of memory versus reconstruction. Were memories really more reliable than reconstruction? Could reconstruction actually take the place of memory, especially if the reconstruction did not lead to further recall. For this patient and for many other patients, reconstruction seemed remote from the present here-and-now interaction of the transference. The "Ah-Hah" reaction to transference interpretations, which is often associated with the lifting of infantile amnesia, was present. For many analysts, the recovery of specific memories is far less important than the patterns elicited in the transference, as Kris (1956c) had emphasized. But there is a different point of view as well, which should not depend upon either Greenacre's (1956) emphasis upon specific memories and reconstruction of actual traumatic experience or Kris's emphasis upon pathogenic patterns and relationships and chronic or cumulative strain trauma. In this point of view, memory was screen memory, highly subjective, fragmented and dislocated, likely distorted, and often misleading in the analytic process. Reconstruction was more accurate than memory or an aggregate of memories. Reconstruction aimed at temporal, logical, developmental sequences—taking into account organizational and phase-transformational propensities. While for some analysts, reconstruction was more speculative and had less conviction than memory, for others reconstruction was actually more reliable and more accurate than memory. Reconstruction integrated the analytic data and the patient's memories in a form which transcended memory alone. In this sense, the reconstruction is always on a higher level of development and organization than discrete memories dating from different temporal and developmental phases of life. The therapeutic benefits to the patient accrue in the reduction of defense, the undoing of fixation and confusion, and in new ego integration, as well as the restoration of continuity of the total personality. Reconstruction would then be far more connected with ego integration and mature structural reorganization, as opposed to being a mere substitute for memory, especially memory of traumatic experience.

The issue of reconstruction in relation to the traditional, crucial analysis of unconscious infantile conflict was also examined. Reconstruction can serve as a stimulus to free association, and when used effectively, to a lessening and loosening of resistance. Reconstruction, for example, in relation to a prototypical use of denial in early childhood, can lead to overcoming a particular type of resistance. This will be followed by the emergence of new material, often confirmatory. Transference interpretations will then proceed with genetic interpretations and then with further reconstruction, all interacting with one another in the analytic process. The interpretation of the patient's voyeurism-exhibitionism, fixation to the primal scene, and denial of what he was seeing in the transference will all be intrinsically related to his unconscious infantile conflicts. As the primal scene becomes even more dangerous, he adopts the feminine role, hides his penis, and so on. But in the patient here described, the fantasied

sadomasochistic aspects of the primal scene were validated, further reinforcing the unconscious fantasy.

The analytic data can be simultaneously understood
through reconstruction upward (Loewenstein, 1951), in
terms of the patient's current conflicts and life situation.
The patient was actually experiencing personal and familial tragedy. When the father was presented, after the crippled brother was born, as "castrated," the patient identified not only father with mother but also father with
brother. The parents might very well have had postpartum depression after the birth of the son with the crippling, congenital anomalies. The aggression toward the
child and guilt over it were reminiscent of the patient's
guilt over his aggression toward the birth of his other
brother and his fears of retaliation. Punitive retaliation
was delayed, but it was now occurring. The patient's infantile and adolescent masturbation were also hypothesized
as contributing to the feeling that he had damaged himself
through transgression. He had "jerked himself off," with
projection of hostility and blame.

In the transference, the patient was being exploited
by the Jewish analyst; Jewish physicians were doing "terrible things to innocent, unsuspecting patients." The history
and the transference supplemented each other. The patient appeared to have been insecure in his masculine
identity and in his personal identity prior to the extraordinary threat to his body self and his objects. He hid under-
neath his mother's skirt with probable merger fantasies.
He had fantasies of the best of both gender worlds as his
own world appeared to be threatened with destruction.
And he was persecuted from within by a progressive illness. His anti-Semitism took on a nearly malignant character. The reconstruction facilitated resolution of the transference. Anti-Semitism was a signal indication of its
dynamic influence and therapeutic power. From the perspective of analytic research and inference, the specific

reconstruction, though acknowledged to be inexact and incomplete, was an inextricable part of a bilaterally illuminating process of reconstruction which would have been continued in further analytic work.

Chapter Five

Childhood Seduction and Contemporary Reconstruction

Ms. A was a single woman in her twenties when she began analysis. In the earlier psychoanalytic literature, she probably would have been described as having experienced seduction trauma. She recalled sexual play with an older man, a neighbor who was psychologically close to the family, her father's best friend, from ages 7 to 11. This was not a discrete shock trauma as had been described by Freud (1896a) in the preanalytic period or in the Wolf Man case (Freud, 1918), but rather, prolonged strain or cumulative trauma. Ms. A's relationship with her neighbor, Mr. Joe, was more like the case of Dora (1905), with her protracted, eroticized, romantic relationship with her father's close friend, Herr K. Although the case has elements of shock trauma, it could be better described in terms of protracted strain, pathogenic object relations, chronic sexual abuse of a child, cumulative trauma, and compensatory reparative behavior. Latency and preadolescence were disrupted, and the analytic data indicate disturbed development in the periods both antecedent and subsequent to the blatant sexual seduction.

Ms. A had been in psychotherapy for many years prior to analysis. Just before she began her psychoanalytic treatment she had become involved with a male drug addict. Much of the analytic work in the first months of the analysis involved her stormy testing of whether she could be tolerated as an analytic patient. She became aware only gradually that her lateness and cancellation of appointments and her tendencies toward sexual promiscuity threatened analytic progress. She had trouble sleeping, as well as getting up in the morning for her sessions, and was angry about what she regarded as analytic demands for her to awaken and attend sessions. She was concerned not only about her masturbation and homosexual preoccupation, but also about what she called "sadistical fantasies"; these were actually masochistic fantasies which dominated her inner life. Feeling humiliated and degraded in her fantasies and by her real-life behavior, she took some pride in being able to denigrate the therapeutic efforts of previous therapists. Very early in the analysis she depicted herself as the innocent victim of that horrible person, her neighbor Mr. Joe, who had inflicted permanent damage by his ongoing sexual seduction during her childhood, ruining her forever.

Although seeing herself as an innocent victim, Ms. A nevertheless described herself as a child prostitute. She explained that she would visit Joe practically every day, and he would give her quarters, candies, and other treats in return for her sexual favors. He would take her into his bedroom where he would masturbate her to an orgastic-type experience. She thought that at one point she had told her family that she was involved with "Joe," and she was taken to see a psychiatrist. Not knowing whether either her parents or the psychiatrist believed her, she was left feeling confused and ashamed.

Ms. A realized that she made every relationship into a replication of that with Mr. Joe, and felt that the seduction experience colored all of her later relationships and preferences. She hesitated to say his name for fear that it would make her sick. When she recalled her childhood memories of Mr. Joe, she felt that she was going to "puke." Thinking about him while sexually aroused with men in her adult life also elicited simultaneous feelings of dismay and disgust.

Concerns about sexual arousal were evident in Ms. A's history and in the transference. She mentioned a magazine article about a study in which photographs were shown to individuals to test the ocular-pupillary reaction to nude figures. Dilation of the pupils would indicate excitement, and she thought the pupils would be more dilated seeing nude women than seeing nude men. She remembered incidents of actually starting to cry and of nausea when someone commented about her being seductive. Mr. Joe had commented to her mother that she was seductive sitting on the floor with her legs apart; and that she was therefore responsible for the relationship, for having seduced him. She frequently related long, complicated dreams in her sessions and soon described a recurrent dream. A wind would pull her down from a staircase in an old house where she would be pulled or sucked through a door or doorway. In her associations she thought that it would be wonderful to be pulled through a keyhole into such a house and to have had such a house for herself when she was a girl. She described her own house, its architecture, and how she would like to clean and modernize it and bring together the best of old and new architecture. The suction in the dream reminded her of tornados, and she wished that the tornado would "just jump up in the dream and land right next to me." Her feelings about the tornado then shifted from wish to fear.

Ms. A then remembered another dream in which she was given a key by someone and at the same time told, "Don't use this key, don't go on the other side of the door." She really wanted to use the key; it was a long key, a skeleton key, and there was a very large keyhole. She opened the door with the key and suction pulled her right in and down the stairs like in the old house in the neighborhood in which she had lived. Unaware of the sexual symbolism, she was afraid of opening the floodgates of emotion and memory. She had previously dreamed about going to the other side of doors, and she remembered the idea that she was breaking a prohibition. This evoked childhood memories. Her mother had imposed many prohibitions, and as soon as her mother told her what not to do, she could hardly wait to do it. After she had been told that she should not go into a particular part of the backyard with her bike, she fell down twenty-five stairs. At the time of her injury she thought her parents and uncle were more concerned about the bike. She recalled some sexual experiences as a child; for example, an occasion when she and a girl friend tied up a boy next door and "tickled him all over." In a similar fashion to Mr. Joe, he would go into his house and obtain candy for her and her girl friend. She would have liked to hide from her father, and was pleased with the idea of having a private place of her own. At the same time, she was afraid of being home alone and would take a knife to bed for self-protection. She soon recognized that she had persisting, highly emotional recollections which she traced back and forth through her childhood, alternating pleasant memories with persistent fears. In sex with Mr. Joe, she had been sucked downward and backward, threatening regressive chaos with terrible injury.

Despite the cumulative traumatic experience and intense conscious and unconscious childhood conflict, Ms. A had also shown some resilience, resourcefulness, and self-righting tendencies. She had come to psychoanalysis with the conscious hope of improving her lot in life and of beneficially changing her personality. She wanted to rewrite the painful past history and wished for a happier ending with analytic help. If she were able to get herself together, she could have beautiful things, including children, animals, and playthings.

Ms. A's hopes for an amelioration of her conflicts, fixations, and regressive vulnerabilities coexisted with a compulsion to repeat. This woman, who between the ages of 7 and 11, had been subjected to frequent, intermittent, high levels of incestuous sexual excitement had, in effect, developed a traumatophilia. She was prone to repeat abusive relationships that were inevitably self-defeating and destructive. Many issues were addressed during the analytic work, and it became evident that the dramatic and traumatic episodes of childhood seduction had as sequelae ego and superego impairment, limiting her capacity to master the repetition of seduction. There was a fantasied blissful peace on the one hand and expectation of an explosive tornadolike experience on the other. A nightmarish quality was recognized beneath the overwhelming tornado forces. This was not only associated with shifts from pleasurable excitement to insufferable states of panic and rage, but also to an internal recognition of abusive exploitation.

Sadomasochistic incestuous wishes to be a prostitute and identifications both as seduced and as a seductive, castrating, murderous prostitute were central fantasies. One outcome of the sexual abuse was her unconscious intention to repeat in life all the overstimulation and misery through unmodulated sadomasochistic relationships. She was consciously hoping for progressive mastery while being afraid of being sucked downward and backward in the regression of analysis into a destructive and self-destructive vortex.

A number of questions now appeared. What had predisposed Ms. A to this pathogenic relationship? Why had she continued the relationship and not been able to free herself to develop along more constructive paths? Was she presenting herself as a seduced victim for defensive purposes? Is the story of the seduction a personal myth (Kris, 1956b), a miscarried effort to reconstruct her own pathogenic experiences in order to explain and rationalize her present difficulties? The latter question of personal myth brought up a closely associated issue of fantasy versus reality. She recalled the skepticism of the psychiatrist and her parents, and some members of the research group were skeptical about the remembered, reported pattern of seduction trauma. It was noted that her presentation of the dramatic and traumatic experience had a quality of reality which was a very important part of her style. Was the patient presenting a Gothic romance and was she seducing her analyst, and now the analytic research group? Would analysts not love to hear about a woman who had been chronically involved in a sexual relationship with an older man when she was between the ages of 7 and 11? Why did it stop at 11, and why didn't it stop sooner?

There was concern that the history of analysis itself was being repeated. Was this a case of seduction trauma as Freud (1896a) first proposed, or a far more complicated type of pathogenesis? This was clearly not simply seduction with cumulative trauma, but entailed a long period of pathogenic object relations, strained and deviant development, and a massive interruption of latency.

From the point of view of reconstruction, the analyst wondered about the reciprocal influence of her fantasy life and her life experience. What had really happened? If it really happened the way it was reported, who was doing what to whom, when, in what way, and for what purposes? Below the surface, what was transpiring in the patient's inner life, her unconscious conflicts and fantasies, her preconscious thoughts and feelings? What was her subjective construction of the seduction? What were the immediate and the long-term sequelae?

There was a convergence of interest in the patient's development prior to the period of seduction in late latency. This was indeed a traumatized, developmentally disordered girl who had sought caregiving from a "friendly" neighbor, had felt betrayed and abused, but had forged a sadomasochistic tie.

The analytic anamnesis and reconstruction of Ms. A's earlier life illuminated her subsequent psychopathology. Of vast importance was the fact that her father was an alcoholic, prone to be both very aggressive and seductive with her. He was temperamental and emotionally labile, with a style of unpredictable, inappropriate behavior. Ms. A was a second daughter, and her father was most unhappy with a second girl, having wanted a son. The analysis revealed that he not only loved to brush Ms. A's hair but also to bathe her, almost up to the age of adolescence. Moreover, her mother not only failed to protect Ms. A from her father's seductive and punitive behavior, but she would also provoke her husband into attacking their daughter. When the father came home from work, the mother would report how terrible the patient's behavior had been, and like the clerical prosecution during the Inquisition, the wicked victim was turned over to the punitive authority for punishment. The patient felt unprotected and relatively rejected by her mother who was often experienced as unempathic, insensitive, and unable to comfort or nurture Ms. A with consistency.

The patient was severely beaten but also became adroit at escaping beatings. The escape was another facet of her hiding in the house behind locked doors and in secret compartments. The patient, not surprisingly, had a highly developed punitive superego and a rather deficient, benevolent, and protective superego. From early childhood, long before the latency seduction, she had a great capacity for feeling guilty, seeking punishment, and feeling remorse for her transgression. She not only felt irrationally guilty, but she did things that justified her sense of guilt; eventually she excelled in self-criticism. She not only recalled trying to escape from beatings, but also regained

95

memories of seeking beatings to relieve her guilt and, through suffering, to atone for having "done something quite terrible." As so often happens, she blamed herself for the abuse by Joe and unconsciously by her parents.

Ms. A's masturbation was associated with both relief and the intensification of conflict and guilt. She had a need to confess, which she did, to her priest. She stressed her masturbation more than the abusive sexual relationship, and this was concordant with the attitude of the priest. To masturbate, she was told, was worse than to have sexual relations. Possibly she was seducing the priest into telling her what she wanted to hear. At the very time she was confessing to masturbation at 13 years of age, she was still being bathed by her father—the same father who could be affectionate and sentimental could suddenly change into a sadistic attacker. She confessed to both more and less than masturbation, but defensively avoided the issue of her sadomasochistic relationship with her parents and between her parents. The term *overstimulation* does not do justice, in terms of analytic understanding, to the variety of pathogenic influences, inappropriate parenting with failure to protect the child, and to her own participation in the intrafamilial, contagious excitement and disturbances. Overt collusion coexisted with unconsciously condoned seduction and punishment. The mother colluded with the father's bathing and beating Ms. A, and Joe's wife condoned Joe's being alone with her in their bedroom. Child abuse was thinly disguised as help with homework.

As the case was first discussed, reconstruction traced Ms. A's style of free association, her transference style and behavior, her dreams and erotic fantasies to the childhood seductive relationship between 7 and 11. A consensus developed that the patient had been overstimulated and burdened with shame and guilt throughout latency. This led to extraordinary maneuvers and an inconsistent, unreliable, harsh supergo. Developmental strain had begun in the preoedipal period and continued through the later phases, including adolescence. In a sense, Ms. A's seducers were her parents and it was they who were the primary partners in seduction, rather than the neighbor. In some respects, the relationship with the neighbor-seducer continued and defended against the seduction and aggressive assaults at home. It was also noted that it was unlikely that a sexual relationship with a man between the child's ages of 7 and 11 had remained static but had undergone its own vicissitudes and changes.

Another hypothesis also came into focus which stressed the importance of the collusion of all parties. In a conspiracy of silence, the patient was unprotected and actually unconsciously encouraged to participate in the sexual seduction with the neighbor who was her father's best friend. The parents shared passive complicity in selling their daughter for "a mess of pottage." The neighbor had offered economic favors to the parents as well as to the daughter, and there were doubtless hidden, unconscious, perverse gratifications in her parents' vicarious exploitation of their daughter. She was a "child prostitute" who had been covertly prostituted by her parents and overtly by their friends.

The collusion among the patient, her sexual partner who was her father's friend, his wife, and the patient's parents were all interrelated and woven into a massive conspiracy of silence. This was an important aspect in the reconstruction of her superego pathology. The silence was related to evasion and confusion of rules and regulations. Ms. A had been bribed by payments of money and candy with resulting superego corruption, readiness to accept superego bribes in the form of "sops to her conscience," regressive vulnerabilities, and reinforcement of the archaic, punitive superego. Her oedipal victory had left her immensely guilty and struggling against feelings of guilt. She had participated, of her own volition, in what amounted to her own sexual molestation or abuse, at least as she consciously recalled, unaware of possible external pressures. Ms. A's experience is consistent with reports of victims of sex abuse as having sought warmth and affection. She was a child who had had an incestuous sexual relationship with an abusive parent surrogate with enormous guilt and shame, with the latent, silent participation of her own parents.

The social and cultural background could not be ignored, and the adult partner must have been aware, on a fully conscious level, of the potential social stigma and the actual illicit nature of the relationship. He knew that what he was doing was not only shameful and could not be revealed, but that he could be subject to arrest and to prosecution. The patient must have sensed her "lover's" guilt and shame, so that her own guilt and shame were increased by identification with the partner's guilt and shame; this notion is related to the concept of borrowed guilt (Freud, 1923). The feeling that her adult partner was "so nice, so tender" was clearly associated with opposite, coexisting, unconscious feelings of hate and loathing, and with conscious self-loathing. There was also an association between the self-loathing and internal condemnation in the form of disgust, nausea, and feeling physically ill upon any sexual encounter in later life. Her sexual relations always involved the fantasied sexual play with her latency adult partner associated with nausea. She recalled her uncomfortable sexual feelings concerning her father who, with her mother's collusion, had bathed her and taught her about "womanhood." She reported also experiencing nausea and a sense of repulsion when she was physically near her father, especially when he was inebriated. Prior to her analysis, the closer she came to any man, the more she felt desperate, with increased closeness and intimacy culminating in sexual frigidity.

It was noted that the patient was very frightened of her aggression, her punitive and self-punitive trends. She was afraid of her hatred leading to destruction of the object. As a young child, she had experienced vengeful fantasies of violently murdering Joe. She was constantly worried about the death of her parents, wishing their death and fearing that the death was surely going to happen. Her punitive superego was a destructive, attacking, inner structure. Her concerns about death were related to both omnipotent aggressive wishes and to omnipotent anticipation, retaliation, and punishment. The patient also had the destructive power of blackmail, the inner knowledge that she could expose the adult partner to prosecution and punishment.

Silent disapproval as well as silent condoning contributed to the burden of silence borne by the patient. The inability to speak about the sordid pathological relationships was incorporated within the syndrome of overstimulation and seduction. The patient's inability to speak to parents who were unable to "hear" her only intensified her shame and guilt and tendencies to denial and dissociation, self-doubt and self-blame. She could not discuss her thoughts and feelings, her subjective experience with its own distortions, or validate the secret, frightening, and exciting reality which remained unacknowledged. Left to her own devices, she could not extricate herself from the pathogenic ties and tended actively and passively to repeat what was unverbalized. The silence, like the guilt, was an immense burden for the child to carry, and the conflicts surrounding her secrecy were later carried into the analytic transference.

Could this patient really free associate, given the long-standing history of secrecy, deception, and a pact of silence? The analytic alliance was initially tenuous and, although the patient had retained some capacities for trust and confidence, her trust had also been betrayed and violated by the authority figures in her life. The reconstruction would have to include the evolution of her unconscious fantasies in relation to how and why the relationship began at age 7, as well as how the seduction secretly proceeded and developed. It was unlikely that the cloak of silence had resulted in a total eclipse of all references to the "incestuous" sexual relationship; rather there must have been a complex set of nonverbal and verbal communications. The child and adults had communicated their intent not to talk about the incestuous behavior, and to conceal the sexual encounters, which were carried out in secrecy and following which, everyone involved, Ms. A. Mr. Joe, Mr. Joe's wife, and Ms. A's parents, behaved as though nothing had happened. The bribery was not only for sexual favors but also to buy silence. The girl had been instructed not to talk about her experiences, and she probably felt that the shame, pain, and punishment she had endured would be compounded by revelation. What was said and left unsaid between the partners, and the patient's identification with parental collusion, contributed to Ms. A's suffering in silence. It was also not clear if she thought she would be believed and anticipated further humiliation and punishment. She suffered in silence but would be shamed and disgraced if she spoke of the seduction and abuse. Since the adults acted as if nothing had happened, their silence favored her own denial in fantasy. This "not knowing what she knew" is frequently combined with a fear of not being believed by external authorities in the "conspiracy of silence."

The case was not one of repression in the classical sense since the seduction was not a repressed, buried trauma. The patient had remembered and ruminated on her childhood sexual relationship with Joe prior to analysis. Suppression and evasion supported the repression of earlier trauma and unconscious oedipal as well as sado-masochistic conflict. The reconstruction in the case reported by Rosen (1953) was relevant, with particular pertinence to the issue of permission to remember, to report, to bear witness. Rosen reconstructed an attempt of a patient's mother to commit suicide from the patient's therapeutic associations and behavior. The patient reacted to this, not as if new material were emerging, but as if the analyst had given him permission to speak about the traumatic situation. The reconstruction in that case was not deeply connected with a repressed event, but rather with parental authority that had demanded suppression of memory and of connection between past and present. A myriad of connections have to be restored in such cases for the patient to grasp the relationship between her fantasies and her life experience and to have a restored sense of the continuity of her personality. In the case of this latency girl, her hearing her father calling her name in relation to the almost daily fondling of her genitals by her father's friend may well have indicated not only incest fantasy and name-calling, but a longing for protection, understanding, and rescue. She yearned for support, nurturance, and safety and for the opportunity to state and name her problems, her seducer, and the nature of her "shameful" sexual activity.

In this case, dreams and transference both were important contributors to the process of reconstruction. As the analysis progressed, the transference took on greater importance. The patient, during the first years of analysis, often began sessions stating that she had had a "very disturbing dream." In the last years of analysis, there were fewer dreams, but the transference was much more clearly present, understandable, and took on dreamlike qualities previously found only in relation to her dreams. As the transference deepened, the patient's longing for maternal care and closeness gradually came to the fore. The patient always had a sleep disturbance and could not cope with any type of separation without severe depression and feelings of desperation. Her aloofness and hostility in relationships also protected her from rejection and separation. The maternal transference with preoedipal coloring came to the fore. She reported a fantasy about making love with a black girl during masturbation, specifically: "The girl and I were dancing nude, and the man whom I had sexual play with was there. He was watching; that was Mr. A; I was being very spiteful, I hurt him." In this primal scene, she attacks father and seeks mother. Early in the analysis she actually had dreamed of being in a brawl with a woman to whom she was attracted, reaching orgasm. She dreamt of nuns who took off their clothes, and superficially represented her own exhibitionism and fear of loss of control. In this dream, the patient turned into an older woman, and the kid who was there looked like an autistic kid. She helped the child beat the nun, wanting to show her that you can express emotion. "But she was lifeless, she was inactive." The patient's self and mother representations were split between nun and prostitute, innocent and guilty. But she also wanted to possess her mother and extract love, and coerce care and nurturance.

It was noted that the patient herself had been fragmented in her life experience and silent and passive about her difficulties. Severe isolation of affect left her feeling lifeless at times and without help or hope. The fact that her adult seducer was depicted as only an observer was also a reversal in which she accused the parents of observing and doing nothing to protect their daughter. The transference was replete with sadomasochistic seduction fantasies and with yearnings for protection and nurturance. There was no doubt that earlier oedipal and preoedipal material was telescoped with latency and later experiences. Repetitive trauma raised many interesting questions concerning the telescoping of past and present and self and objects with considerable confusion and interidentification. There was a tendency toward both splitting of representations and confusion of the motives, feelings, and reactions of self and "seducer" (Shengold, 1989). Repetitive and cumulative trauma had set off chain reactions with reverberations and ramifications in many different directions. Earlier traumas were then condensed with the later experiences. In certain respects, the reconstruction was concerned with the sequential, intrapsychic connections which, from genetic and developmental points of view, bound the later experiences to the earlier ones. The reconstruction aimed at tracing back a chain of connected relationships, linking otherwise isolated antecedents, and, where possible, demonstrating cause and effect. The analytic data are ordered to get a better picture of the patient's developmental progression and reorganization of her personality as it occurred during the various developmental phases. Developmental considerations superseded psychosexual phase specificity in overall importance. Reconstruction garnered analytic evidence that the "mutual" seduction in latency, so important in its own pathogenicity, also served as a defense, in part, against the prelatency traumas and personality disturbance. The nuns were a defensive bulwark against sexuality, a protective place where she could escape. The nuns were idealized, asexual mothers representing morality and safety.

The oedipal transference explained much of the patient's childhood seduction, on a daily basis, from ages 7 to 11, bribed by candy and coins. But the transference hinted at a highly disguised pleading and crying for a nurturant, protective mother. Her object and affect hunger for maternal care and nurturance was reconstructed as the foundation for her perverse oedipal seduction and her desperate need to be desired, fondled, and indulged. In her hostile, maternal transference she held her mother responsible for the deprivation and for the later sexual abuse. Related to the homosexual transference, this specific reconstruction of her preoedipal and negative oedipal regressive vulnerability to seduction was a major contribution to analytic understanding and progress.

In summary, this case demonstrated the complexity and overdetermination of a pathogenic sexual relationship which continued through latency. There was developmental disturbance preceding and during latency and then continuing into adolescence. In this case, the almost daily fondling by her adult neighbor was not associated with coercion or violence, but the long duration of the abuse increased the propensity for greater harm. The patient "cooperated" with conscious complicity and with her own hidden and overt childish gratifications. The case did not directly involve overt incest with a member of her family. The incestuous seduction, however, involved her parents as "coconspirators" with the adult neighbor. The immature latency child could not possibly entirely comprehend the nature of the "seduction" as sexual molestation or give adult informed consent. She also unconsciously reacted to the guilt, shame, and fear of exposure and prosecution of her adult partner. There was no single or simple etiology or traumatic factor. The child was not simply gratifying oedipal wishes, but was exploited for the wishes and defenses of caretakers. Moral and social scruples were violated, and body as well as generational boundaries were breached, with "somatic imprints" in the psyche (Kramer, 1990).

What was once described as seduction trauma is now understood in an intrapsychic but also a developmental and familial context. The traumatic experience occurs during a particular developmental phase, or overlapping phases, influenced by the child's ego state, fantasy life, object relations, and the child's constitutional endowment and further experience (Levine, 1990). The traumatized child will identify with victim and aggressor, rescuer and comforter, so that identifications are important in both the fixation to trauma and the mastery of trauma (Blum, 1987). Real experience will influence the strength, form, and content of fantasies which press for repetition; real experience thus codetermines psychic reality (Greenacre, 1956). The tendency to reenact inside and outside the analytic transference may need special analytic attention and may elicit parameters or technical modifications.

There is no specific symptom or syndrome that is a sequela of childhood sexual abuse. While some patients may become inhibited and obsessively indecisive, others clearly show repetition in action, whether in promiscuity, perversion, or abusive or punitive parenthood. Some martinets punish children because of projected guilt and blame for their own conscious and unconscious incestuous transgressions. It should be noted that throughout history and cross-culturally, children have been subject to all manner of punishment for masturbation (Blum, 1989). The child is punished for the caretaker's real and fantasied transgressions while also gratifying the child's self-punitive and masochistic tendencies. The superego of the abused child will be impaired with both overly permissive and cruelly punitive trends.

The sequela of this type of cumulative trauma and developmental disruption requires transference analysis and careful, protracted reconstruction for full comprehension. There are some characteristic developmental and structural consequences, if not characteristic symptomatic phenomena.

Basic trust is impaired, and this patient and others experienced relative maternal deprivation and lack of protection and empathy. The patient could be confused about how and what really happened; reality takes on imaginary qualities, and fantasy may appear to be real. Children may be particularly confused about their own internal passion and wishes and external seduction or coercion. Unconscious conflict and fantasy are validated and anchored in traumatic reality with enduring effects upon the personality. Denial, doubting, and dissociation, cognitive and affective disturbance, with ego splitting in more malignant cases, are significant sequelae (Shengold, 1989). The splitting into idealized and devalued representations of self and object adds to ego weakness and dysfunction. The abused child may later feel like an exception, entitled to special privileges as both a victim and an oedipal victor. It is a pyrrhic victory with demands for punishment and self-punishment. An entrenched victim position may result in demands for restitution, reparation, and revenge, or for the confession, contrition, and apology of the abuser. Demands for justice and compensation may individually help or hinder mourning, and progressive mastery of trauma. Victimization tends to be enacted and/or inflicted on others, including the next generation.

All the major calamities of childhood are intensified: castration anxiety, loss of the object's love (plus loss of self-esteem), and loss of the object. Regression, as a defense and to points of traumatic fixation, is commonly observed, and regression may be a specific vulnerability. Areas of developmental arrest and deviation may be complicated by regressive alteration. Depressive reactions are probably ubiquitous. There may be a need to mourn losses and idealized illusions and objects. This patient's sadomasochistic disposition was probably consolidated in latency, with oedipal deformation. Her compulsion to repeat and to enact her central sadomasochistic fantasies was rooted in serial strain trauma, pathogenic object relations and identifications, and extended, extensive developmental disorder. The case raises many interesting questions concerning the reconstruction of psychic reality, of actual experience, and the reconstruction of developmental phase disturbance, sequence, and sequelae.

In this case, as in similar protracted childhood sexual seductions, the organizing and disorganizing effects are not due to discrete shock traumas. The entire developmental period of the seduction has an organizing effect upon subsequent development, and the task of reconstruction is far more complicated than the pioneer psychoanalytic reconstruction of a primal scene or other discrete childhood sexual trauma.

Further, the actual analytic attitude and role of the analyst is significant. Does the analyst remain neutral, consistent, reliable, or subject to countertransference reactions? Are technical departures necessary where there has been structural damage or developmental arrest? For the analyzable patient, it did not seem that psychotherapeutic measures were necessary and even a modified analysis could be very helpful. The analyst is also a new object, and as analysis proceeds, is differentiated more from the original objects. Whether the analyst can and does serve as a "primary object" in renewed development, especially where conflict and trauma are associated with developmental and structural deficit, needs further research. This issue was not elucidated in this case which was analyzed by standard technique and in which ego disturbance was alleviated by the analysis of conflict and trauma.

The question of validating or believing the report of the incestuous or abusive experience is less significant where it is patterned and remembered over a long period of time, at a later stage of childhood and adolescent development. However, whether remembered or repressed, recent or remote, such childhood or adolescent sexual maltreatment requires detailed analytic reconstruction of the patient's intrapsychic experience and functions and the interplay of psychic and external reality. Even just after a child has been molested, the recent experience will already be subject to ego confusion and defensive alteration. The subjectivity of memory means that reconstruction is required. Reconstruction is essential to the attenuation of unconscious conflict and cumulative trauma and the reorganization of developmental disorder. The reconstruction of this patient's disordered latency and prelatency was essential to her beneficial analytic treatment.

The countertransference is a very important consideration in such a case of childhood seduction. The analyst's dedication, neutrality, and integrity will be tested. The analyst initially should neither accept nor deny the patient's own report and constructions. The analyst may overreact to the patient and to her seductive objects, as well as to moral, ethical, and legal issues. For purposes of reconstruction, the term *countertransference* has to be understood in its broad sense, which is more than irrational, unconscious reactions to the patient's transference. "Countertransference" or counterreaction to reconstruction involves the analyst's attitude toward the patient's past, the analyst's own past, and the analyst's preferences, prejudices, and theoretical predilections concerning reconstruction. In this specific type of patient, the analyst should not be seduced by the patient's seductiveness and tendencies toward erotized transference. Nor should the analyst be seduced into incorrect reconstruction with overtones of blame or continued victimization. Sexually abused patients may be highly seductive and vengeful, repeating the pathogenic relationships, albeit in a safe and ethical analytic situation. If "seduction trauma" is bilaterally acted out in the transference-countertransference and abuse repeated in treatment, it is more likely when both patient and therapist have a similar history of (severe) childhood trauma. The repetition avoids painful recollection, attempts oedipal victory and active control, and destroys the analyst's authority and the analytic process.

Chapter Six

Analysis of a Five-Year-Old: Reconstruction in the Child Analytic Process

This case is presented in order to demonstrate and elucidate transference issues in child analysis. Transference developments were not limited to current reactions to the original love objects, but included infantile strivings, reanimated by the analytic process, and directed toward the analyst. A limited, circumscribed transference neurosis centered on the analyst and the analytic situation as is sometimes evident during periods of treatment with young children. As a revival and recapitulation of the past, the transference is a rich source of data which may be used for reconstruction. However, reconstruction depends upon the totality of analytic data and not upon any one type of material such as transference or dreams.

The case had not been analyzed with particular emphasis or interest in reconstruction so that there was no built-in bias toward or against reconstruction in the analytic data. There had been no specific research goal, and the reconstructions made during the course of the analysis were a spontaneous part of the analytic work. The analysis had been conducted some years ago, and the analyst's own views concerning reconstruction and transference in child analysis had changed over the years with more experience and greater knowledge. Further, the analyst's knowledge of child development had been greatly enriched by the findings of Mahler and others who had contributed so much to advances in developmental knowledge (Mahler, Pine, and Bergman, 1975). The role of reconstruction in the analytic process doubtless would have been different if the case were one of contemporary psychoanalysis. Given the advantages and disadvantages, there was a strong feeling that the detailed clinical material derived from an excellently conducted child analysis could be adapted and utilized for an in-depth investigation of reconstruction. Perhaps because it was a child case, there was more concern from the outset about differentiating a reconstructive framework from the child analytic process as a whole than about differentiating between reconstruction and genetic interpretation.

Having a child case brings us closer to the developmental process, but that does not necessarily make reconstruction any easier. The pathogenesis of symptom and character, the evolution of the child's ego strengths and resources, may or may not be available in the analysis of a young child. So many paths and possibilities are opened developmentally that predictions of adult attitudes, character, and sublimations are rather hazardous. At the same time, genetic reconstruction imposes an impression of genetic continuity. Freud (1920b) noted,

> So long as we trace the development from its final outcome backwards, the chain of events appears continuous, and we feel we have gained an insight which is completely satisfactory or even exhaustive. But if we proceed the reverse way, if we start from the premises inferred from the analysis and try to follow these up to the final result, then we no longer get the impression of an inevitable sequence of events which could not have been otherwise determined.

We notice at once that there might have been another result, and that we might have been just as well able to understand and explain the latter. The synthesis is thus not so satisfactory as the analysis; in other words, from a knowledge of the premises we could not have foretold the nature of the result [p. 167].

Confronted with an adult female hysteric in psychoanalysis today, analysts wish to know what the seductive, histrionic, exhibitionistic female "looked like" when she was a girl. Was she coy, seductive, charming, and engaging in early latency? Was she really rather shy, distant, and cautious, with a seductive facade added to her character structure at adolescence? What character traits were continuous and which were discontinuous?

The ego immaturity of the child raises questions about the capacity to engage in, understand, and utilize reconstruction of the past (Kennedy, 1971). The child "lives" very much in the present and has difficulty differentiating the recent past, let alone the far more remote past of infancy. The child has a very different sense of time and of temporal sequence, interval, and duration than the adult. The child has different concepts of reality and causality, and lacks the logical capacities of the adult. Even though the child has advanced from primary process to secondary process, the level of cognitive organization is not as advanced as it is in the adults. Language will develop further in organization and complexity. The child not only has difficulty in free associating, but also in putting many thoughts and feelings into words. Affects will further develop, and the child is still learning to differentiate, recognize, and express affect in words.

Contemporary reconstruction of self and object representations may be influenced by the child analyst's contact with the original objects. Generally a plethora of developmental data has been provided by parents prior to the inception of analysis. From the point of view of reconstruction, to what degree was this contact with the parents and the knowledge gleaned from them, beneficial or detrimental? Did parents stimulate and facilitate reconstruction or did they introduce distortions, bias, and premature conceptualizations? Comparing the reconstruction in child analysis with that of adult patients was of particular interest since analytic patients change representations of their objects and attitudes toward them as analysis proceeds. These changes are a part of normal development in childhood as well. This aspect of reconstruction concerned with self and object representations, for example, is very different from the reconstruction of traumatic events in the pioneer period of psychoanalysis. Since development in childhood is ongoing and partially ongoing in the analytic process and situation itself, the analyst becomes of special importance not only as transference object but as a real new object. Aspects of new development may first appear in the analytic situation, only to be enacted at home with the "original" objects. At the same time, what happens with the original objects may be repeated in the analytic situation. A full-fledged transference neurosis, except in limited forms and phases of analysis, is not expected in child analysis. Therefore, reconstruction in child analysis might be less dependent upon transference than upon other analytic data as compared with adult analysis. In the case presented here, the transference manifestations were quite significant to the issues of reconstruction. The genetic roots of transference repetition are elaborated by reconstruction, but it belongs to the extratransference sphere of intervention and explanation.

The treating analyst had a number of questions and conjectures early in the analysis concerning "what happened" to the child as well as "when" and "how" it had occurred. What was the child's internal experience of the external events surrounding the sibling's birth, and how would that influence later development? As the analytic process developed, the preliminary constructions in the analyst's mind gradually evolved into specific reconstructions which were to be shared with the child. The reconstructions were important to the analyst's own cohesive understanding of that particular child's difficulties, conflicts, defenses, and characterological tendencies. Different from any single genetic interpretation, the reconstructions functioned to fill in gaps and to provide explanations as to how the child reacted to and shaped the experiences of her life. Children inevitably invent theories or pseudo-reconstructions which represent their own rationalized, edited, explanatory notions and fantasy elaborations. These explanatory efforts, usually of a highly defensive character, are related to issues of screen memories and personal as well as familial myths. Gaps in understanding are filled in with fantasy distortion. Analysis not only lifts repression and recovers memories, but reorganizes the patterning of memory and fantasy; analysis substitutes analytic reconstruction for infantile fantasy construction.

A was 5 years old when her parents accepted the recommendation for analysis. The decision to start analysis had been influenced more by A's passive resignation and compliance than her phobia and tendencies toward feces retention. The transference illuminated the unconscious conflicts behind the pathogenic characterological tendencies as well as her symptoms and anxiety. However, reconstruction had an important role in the analytic process. First, the analyst's reconstructions facilitated both the analytic process and the analyst's own insights. Second, as the analysis unfolded, reconstruction contributed to the therapeutic effect of the child's analysis and to the child's enlarged self-knowledge and understanding of her problems and her relationships.

Four areas of reconstruction were successively introduced and discussed from clinical and theoretical perspectives in the course of the research deliberations: (1) The intrapsychic experience of mother's pregnancy and the birth of the patient's sister when the little girl was 2 years of age, and the patient's reaction to it; (2) the relationship of the child's masturbation and her unconscious masturbation fantasy to her feeling castrated and defective; (3) the role of primal scene experience and fantasy; the organizing role of primal scene trauma and significance of primal scene fantasy in development; and (4) the enema trauma and evidence of coercive tendencies in the parent–child relationship were investigated. It was of particular interest that there was a virtual consensus that the reconstructions were not a flight from the here-and-now of the transference. Contrary to critical voices within the analytic community, the process of reconstruction did not serve and fortify analytic resistance. Inappropriate reconstruction could impede analysis, but the careful, tactful reconstructions here enriched and deepened the analytic process. The child continued to live very much in the present but, particularly as she advanced into middle latency, she could begin to understand her present disturbance in the light of the past, as well as her past as colored by ongoing issues with her parents and sibling.

At certain times in analysis, with certain patients, it was noted that there was almost a necessity to reconstruct, as if the material were crying for reconstruction. This is not true with all patients and certainly not with all analysts. Not all patients are accessible to the process of reconstruction or could be in touch with past feelings, attitudes, and relationships. There was also some disagreement about a model in which the reconstruction of ever earlier pathogenic material is important for therapeutic effect versus attention to later ego organizations and later conflict presentations which might be more therapeutically accessible. Perhaps the gifted analytic patient oriented toward "remembrance of things past," and whose ego functions are especially well endowed in perception, memory, and integration may be far better able to participate in the process of analytic reconstruction. Such patients and their analysts would not be likely to overlook the current context and its contribution to the shape of recrudescent conflict and the form and content of memory. But these patients would be presumably far better able to understand the shaping influence of early life. In the case of this child, her interest in her past life, whether the past analytic session or the remote time when her sibling was born, was very much influenced by the current context of the analysis, her current developmental phase, and her current life experience.

There was a recognition that the reconstruction of A's response to the birth of her sibling could only be approximated, but specific evidence facilitated the reconstruction of sibling hostility and jealousy. There was also recognition that the experience of the sibling's birth on an intrapsychic level had been absorbed into larger patterns and had been amalgamated with later developmental issues and unconscious conflicts. The group debated the old controversy of the specific event and the patterned sequence (Greenacre, 1956; Kris, 1956c). The current controversy of the narrative versus historical truth had probably always been present in psychoanalytic thought in terms of issues of psychic and material reality. To what degree did child and adult analysts attach importance to the reconstruction of actual external events, to the child's internal experience of these events, and to the relationship and coordination or mutual influence of the internal and external? For many analysts, it was not easy to separate the internal and external because of such processes as projection, introjection, denial, and developmental transformations. While the developmental history provided by the parents may be valuable, it cannot be regarded as unbiased and objective.

The plethora of fantasy material raised the question of A's fantasy representations versus the actual mother–child relationship. A initially related to the analyst in terms of the delegation of magical omnipotence; the analyst was a protector, but this could change with the projection of omnipotent aggression. This led to intense discussions concerning the protective, benevolent, and magically restorative mother, as well as the witch mother and the attacking, castrating, evil mother. When and how had the girl split the maternal relationship into good and bad? The analyst had interpreted the splitting of ambivalence, at first indirectly, without immediate reliance upon the transference implications. The analyst's "story" explained "make believe" that the little girl had two mommys—a good one and a bad one, so that the child did not have to worry about being angry at the good mommy whom she loved. The bad mommy could be sent away or be killed, and the girl would still have the good mommy with her. In the analyst's story, the little girl had only one mommy who was the same good mommy whom she loved, but who also sometimes seemed like a bad mommy. Maybe the little girl worried because she got angry at the mommy whom she also loved. A exclaimed, with a knowing smile, "A half-and-half mommy, and a half-and-half child." She laughed uproariously, repeated "half-and-half" several times and wondered, "Wouldn't it be funny to have just half a mommy left." She seemed to be assimilating the analyst's interpretive comment that all people have good and bad.

In the discussion, it was noted that these connections and the interpretation of the child's ambivalence were not yet reconstruction. This was because reconstruction depended upon the connection between the internal response with the specific, evocative external events, the specific internal reactivity, and effects on further psychic functioning and developmental sequences. The analytic question of "what happened" refers to both the actual external situation and the intrapsychic internal response. Unconscious fantasy and conflict does not arise in a vacuum, but external events alone do not tell us enough about the child's internal experience. A child may feel guilty about the birth of a sibling because of murderous hostility toward the sibling and parent; the child's reaction would also be influenced by the parents, feeling threatened by the older child's regression or feeling unable to cope with two children at one time. In addition, it was noted that there are certain dispositional elements: cognitive, affective, and sensory modalities which may lead more ordinary experiences to assume traumatic proportions. This may be highly individual, and the vulnerability may be phase-specific or cut across all the developmental phases. These internal factors interweave with external factors, such as a mother's intensifying a sibling rivalry because of a particular child being a favorite or a threat.

At the time the analysis had started, A was noted to be in the phallic phase, with many unresolved preoedipal issues and without yet having become anchored in oedipal development. Her fears of aggression were to lead more and more in the direction of her masturbatory wishes and activities and the conflicts and defenses associated with her masturbation. The analyst had pointed out, in her words, the feelings that went with her bad thoughts and her need to do something very good to make up for anything she thought she might have done that was bad. For example, there was evidence that the child blamed herself for the analyst's absence (due to a back condition) and was simultaneously worried that the analyst might have forgotten about her little patient. Angry thoughts might have caused the analyst's sore back, and the little girl, who had broken the toy dog's leg, had a need to punish herself by hurting her own leg. The fear of bodily injury emerged more clearly as the girl climbed on high shelves in the playroom to show that she was tempted to undertake dangerous activities. She referred to fires of excitement and to turning on the electric lights and electric heater. She asked if the eraser would come off the pencil if she rubbed too hard. She could perform magical tricks with her hand, and this was also related to the missing amputated hand of Captain Hook and its reassuring as well as threatening replacement in the Peter Pan story.

No decisive reconstruction had yet been given, but it was on the way. The masturbation theme and the theme of sibling birth would become linked together. The child fantasied that she was a messy, dirty, nasty, masturbating child. She was not only punitively castrated, and castrated herself, but also felt unloved and undesirable when replaced by her younger sibling. Captain Hook was the phallic and castrated mother whom the patient had to control. At one point when time was up, the child said that the analyst was Captain Hook and she was gagged and could not talk. She "couldn't tell me to leave." The reconstruction took into account her omnipotent wishes, thoughts, and gestures in the context of her current phallic phase castration conflicts. When the omnipotence is delegated, the analyst is the source of all injuries as well as the source of repair, restoration, and undoing of all injuries. In time, less fearful of injury, the little girl could express her hatred toward her mother and could state that she could kill her analyst and the analyst's little dog.

As might be anticipated, the masturbatory material was also linked to primal scene fantasy and experience. The bunny that didn't go to sleep but covered himself up was the child awake during the primal scene. The reconstruction of the primal scene itself in terms of fantasy and/or reality depends upon the nature of the child's actual primal scene experience, developmental phase, ego organization, and object relations. It is certainly very different if the child is in the bedroom of the parents, if this "sleep-ing arrangement" extends over a number of years, or, as in this case, if the child has been intermittently exposed. A was sometimes awake; sometimes only partially asleep; the bedroom door sometimes open and sometimes closed. A, abandoned to her own excitement, was of course in a different situation than other children more directly in-volved in the parents' sexual relationship and often brought into the situation by the parents' unconscious fan-tasies and needs. There is a difference between primal scene fantasy and primal scene reality. Participation in real primal scenes becomes a form of incestuous perversion. There are differences between primal scene exposure to animals or to strangers or to more distant relatives versus incestuous involvement with parents or grandparents. The reaction of parents, such as startle, shame, anger, compassionate or punitive responses, varies a great deal. In this case, the parents seemed to have denied that they were exposing their daughter to the primal scene (Esman, 1973; Blum, 1979). Their role in the voyeuristic–exhibitio-nist enactment seemed to be outside of their conscious awareness.

The inferences drawn from this child analytic case transcended the significant technical utilization of recon-struction, which facilitated the analytic process, overcom-ing resistance and infantile regression. It assisted in wid-ening the child's insight and ego dominance. Recon-struction reestablished severed connections and also forged new links between past and present, fantasy and reality. Enlarging the child's insight, it also strengthened the therapeutic alliance and the child's interest and under-standing rather than mere alleviation of distress and symptomatic relief. Self and object representations could be remodeled pari passu with the analysis of unconscious infantile conflict and traumas. But as old representations and patterns were in the process of a maturing revision, the reconstructions themselves could be seen as intrinsically interrelated and tending to coalesce.

The enema experience, the coercive toilet training, the father's participation in holding her down, the preoedipal antecedents of castration through weaning and loss of feces, the birth of the sibling, and the child's loss of her privileged position as only child, the constellation of factors associated with her masturbatory activities and fantasies, her primal scene exposure—virtually all the major themes of the analysis were brought together in the reconstructions. The process of reconstruction grew out of a well-defined and well-conducted analytic process. Explanations were mutually illuminating and synergistic as in the child feeling castrated, bad, and dirty—all significantly related to her subjective experience of the birth of her sibling. The reconstructions were related to the analytic resolution of her dog phobia and her fear of flushing the toilet, as well as to her attitudes of compliance and passive resignation. The child was inhibited and constricted by the fear of her own aggression, and these problems were intensified in the context of coercive, infantile, object relations.

Discussion of later aspects of the child's analysis also led to consideration of trauma as a screen. Traumas of later childhood and later life may be significant in their own right, and not only because of linkage to and reactivation of infantile traumas. In some cases, more significant later trauma may be disguised and defended by the manifest reanimation of earlier traumatic experience.

Greenacre (1956) observed that the acting out in later childhood, under the compulsion to repeat, of an earlier untoward experience, may prove more disturbing and evoke more guilt because it has been actively precipitated by the child and because superego development by then is more advanced; the earlier disturbing experience now screens the later and more disturbing one.

In A's third year of analysis the analyst reconstructed that at age 3 she had been left alone with her baby sister. She had been overwhelmed by panic arising from her fear of losing control over her hostile impulses directed against the little intruder and from her terror lest her mother abandon her because of these impulses. In the fifth year of her analysis, when she was 9, A was given permission to baby-sit for a neighbor. "Accidentally on purpose," as children versed in the ways of analysis are prone to say, she bumped the baby's head, whereupon he burst into loud, frantic crying. A became terrified, phoned her mother at work, and implored her to come to the apartment where she was baby-sitting. When the mother arrived she found A crouched in the corner, white and trembling—a posture she had assumed at the time of the original experience with her sibling. It is significant that the child spoke of the earlier experience in her analysis before she was able to speak of this more recent one. One may wonder in what order these two events would have emerged had this patient come to analysis as an adult.

The issue of distorting and screening influences in reconstruction highlighted the dynamic interrelationship between past and present. Not only is the present shaped and influenced by antecedent experience, but later influences, accretions, and transformations may alter the significance of past events and experience. Rather than a single pathogenic influence, overdetermination and mutual, multiple influences are the rule. Reconstruction must take into account the complementary aspects of the genetic and developmental points of view (Kennedy, 1971). A. Freud (1951) noted:

> One traumatic prohibition or punishment, remembered or reconstructed, becomes the representative of hundreds of frustrations which had been imposed on the child; one long separation from the mother takes over the combined

effect of innumerable times when the infant has been left alone in his cot, his room, at bedtime, etc. [p. 157].

Reconstruction furthers and expands the analytic process. The approximate reconstruction is remodeled in the course of analytic work and tested against its intrapsychic fit and its articulation with all of the analytic data. Though reconstruction was compared to Glover's (1955) inexact interpretation, "approximate" does not mean incorrect, or misleading, or ineffective. In A's case, the reconstruction of the traumatic experience, for example, of her sister's birth, was compelling. And there was a sense of conviction about this on the part of the treating analyst as well as among virtually all the analysts in the research group. The process of reconstruction is imbedded in the analytic process where "the past emerges into the present, and a readiness, a 'need' for reconstructive interpretations may be noticed" (Kris, 1956c, p. 59).

The reconstruction is subject to its own working through and becomes part of working through in the analysis. It is inevitably a blend of the old and the new, drawing upon the past, but always offering a novel integration of elements that were not and could not have been integrated in that form in early childhood (Cohen, 1980). This integrated insight (Blum, 1979; Neubauer, 1979) promotes further ego development in the child while allowing distance from and understanding of infantile conflict and trauma. Analytic verbalization provides a cognitive–linguistic organization which tends to lift the child's level of experiential organization. Analytic verbalization promotes new integration from its higher levels of reflection, communication, and comprehension. The child's own receptive and expressive language may be an important aspect of the assimilation of reconstruction, especially since it tends to be of greater order of complexity than interpretation. The child has an active role in reconstructive effort commensurate with his or her ego development. Freud's (1937) remarks are also pertinent to child analysis: "The analyst finishes a piece of construction and communicates it to the subject of the analysis so that it may work upon him; he then constructs a further piece out of the fresh material pouring in upon him" (p. 260).

Since children may be more impressed, more easily swayed, or overthrown by authority figures than adults, and because of a child's greater dependency and need for the approval of a parent surrogate, inexact interpretation may carry inappropriate conviction. The ultimate test of reconstruction is not the enthusiasm of the analyst or the patient but the explanatory reach of the reconstruction and its appropriate logical, cohesive, and coherent position in the analytic process and in the analytic data. Differences of opinion and the choice among alternative variations of reconstruction were valuable to maintain open-mindedness, scientific skepticism, and an avoidance of premature closure of very complicated questions. A specific reconstruction can provide an excellent fit and integration of the analytic evidence without resolution of every fine detail. The overarching reconstruction (e.g., of guilt and punishment for aggressive wishes against a sibling) will nevertheless retain conviction and clinical application.

In this connection, reconstructions of the past in the analytic and child analytic literature were subjected to new critical examination. Reconstruction of the experience of a child who had witnessed the murder of her mother by her father (Bergen, 1958) was open to very serious question. That the child was traumatized by the mother's apprehensive rebuke or rejecting statement rather than by witnessing the mother's murder, and experiencing the loss of both parents, in retrospect, were incomplete and probably incorrect reconstructions. The reexamination of accepted or even authoritative reconstructions, which had an influence upon subsequent psychoanalytic thought, was an outgrowth of the research and a stimulus for questioning of the process and content of reconstruction in the case of A. The reconstructed child was not preferred to the analytically observed child, but child analysis, developmental theory, child observation, and reconstruction were synergistic.

The child analysis of A demonstrated that she could be helped to gain interest and insight into her inner fantasy life and to be curious about cause and effect, and how her past experience was significant for her present life. She differentiated past and present, identified with the analyst's observing ego, and appeared to engage and utilize reconstruction. She understood genetic interpretation and reconstruction on her own developmental level which facilitated new ego integration and developmental advance.

Although the parents provided developmental data relevant to reconstruction and the analyst met the parents and learned about their lives and interaction, the actual process of reconstruction was with the child. A. could not remember her infancy and could not independently connect her analytic work with her current home life or her recent or remote past. The distorted fantasies of the child and the child's subjective version of history are used by the analyst in conjunction with the historical manifest content provided by the parents, in this case, especially by the mother.

As A. developed during the years of analysis she could better communicate and connect her fantasy play with her current life at home and in school. Parental advice was kept to a minimum, and the child's confidentiality was maintained despite some minimal continuing contact with her mother. A.'s secrets, fantasies, and transference reactions emerged in her analysis, and the reconstruction of her masturbation guilt and fantasy of castration and mutilation was within and consequent to the analytic process. Reconstruction was part of the child analytic process and further contributed to the analysis of A.'s defenses, attitudes, interests, and her object relations and intrafamilial adaptation. The child analyst could understand the pathogenesis of A.'s disorder—how and why she was disturbed. Reconstruction for the analyst was also an orientation regarding her unconscious infantile conflicts, her transference repetitions, and their genetic interpretation. Analyst and child could shape and share the new experience of the reconstructed past.

This modeling of the reconstruction depends upon the analytic process, though in child analysis, it may incorporate and articulate with data provided by the parents. As an empathic, understanding object, the analyst guides the formulation and application of genetic interpretation and reconstruction. The child's participation varies with maturation, ego development, and psychopathology, and the analyst facilitates ego orientation to causal, temporal, and developmental sequence to a greater degree than is usual in adult analysis. Reconstruction may also paradoxically appear to invite regression while facilitating the child's progressive development. The progressive, integrative aspects of reconstruction converge with the child's tendencies to resume and "complete development." Further, the analyst and analytic situation provide the safety, security, and reliability for the reconstruction of trauma. In addition to the critical, affective understanding obtained, the child's "worst fears" are not realized but disspelled. Development and reorganization may proceed in the presence of and identification with the nonpathogenic new object.

Reconstruction in child analysis is more variable in scope, depth, and distance from the present than in adult analysis. The child analyst may reconstruct to and from home and school, from session-to-session, from present to past conflicts, and from the very recent to the more remote phases of development. Reconstruction may have a lesser role in a particular child analysis, but not necessarily for the analyst. The child analyst requires reconstruction as part of analytic work, illuminating transference, counter-transference, and pathogenesis.

Chapter Seven

Reconstruction, Psychic Reality, and History

The history of reconstruction has always been intertwined with the reconstruction of history. Freud began his psychoanalytic work with a reconstruction of traumatic events in childhood which were persistently pathogenic influences into adult life. These pathogenic traumatic events could be recovered in analytic work with adults, many years after they took place. Accurate, complete memories of the entire traumatic situation were rarely obtained, but reconstruction could be accomplished from the symptomatic derivatives, the patient's neurotic behavior, dreams, and fantasies. The symptoms themselves came to be regarded as fragmented memories. Breuer and Freud (1895, p. 7) noted, *"Hysterics suffer mainly from reminiscences."* Despite the incorrect reconstruction of the universality of childhood seduction trauma as a causative agent of adult psychoneurosis, the role of childhood has remained fundamentally important in clinical psychoanalysis and in psychoanalytic theory. In the early years of psychoanalysis it was assumed that an understanding of the patient's childhood would be essential to the comprehension of his or her personality disorder. Analyst and patient would want to understand the person's childhood in order to know how areas of the patient's personality remained childish, or the role traversed in life to become that particular person within his own family and culture, and when, how, and why the patient had become disturbed. Analytic reconstruction deepened and amplified understanding of how unresolved childhood conflicts and trauma continued to have a pathogenic influence on the adult patient's present life (Greenacre, 1981; Furst, 1986). In this view, the present could not be understood without the distorting influence of the past being taken into account. It was assumed that there was a real factual past and actual life history which would unfold in the analytic work. In this sense, an analytic autobiography would replace a distorted biography in which the patient had rewritten his own history and created his own myths and legends (Kris, 1956b). Analytic work would also remove infantile amnesia, and expose the screening of memory (Reider, 1953). In modern analysis, the recovery of traumatic memories has been replaced by the analysis of unconscious conflict, usually as organized in unconscious fantasy with innate and experiential influences (Arlow, 1991).

Beginning with the realization of incorrect reconstruction by the analyst, as well as by the patient, subjective and relativist elements were introduced into controversies about reconstruction. Was reconstruction objective or subjective, fact or fiction, historical truth or narrative truth? Was reconstruction based upon rational and scientific or adultomorphic, specious assumptions and considerations? Freud, at various times, emphasized both psychic reality and external reality. At different times, he focused upon the power and importance of unconscious fantasy, and he remarked (Freud, 1916–1917) that in the world of the neuroses, psychic reality was far more important than material reality.

In later years, in *Civilization and Its Discontents* (1930), "Constructions in Analysis" (1937), and *Moses and Monotheism* (1939), for example, Freud returned to the importance of actual occurrences. Even his formulation of phylogenetic memories was related to proposed prehistoric events. There is no question that some of the seductions and other traumas reported by patients, had sometimes not occurred, but in most cases there was an admixture of fantasy and reality, which made the work of analysis more difficult and sometimes left the analyst on uncertain ground (Freud, 1916–1917). In his case histories, Freud repeatedly reconstructed actual childhood scenes, often of a traumatic nature. Still using the archaeological model, he carefully reconstructed the seduction scene by the lake that took place when Dora was an adolescent, and her childhood exposure to the primal scene, which he related to her symptoms of dyspnea. He reconstructed the Rat Man's oedipal phase masturbation and childhood seductions in relation to adult fantasies of punishment for oedipal wishes. The Rat Man expected reproach and punishment from his father's ghost, like Hamlet, when engaging in phallic mirror exhibitionism and masturbatory play as an adult instead of diligent work and study. Freud saw this as a thinly disguised repetition of the infantile situation. Although Freud (1909) did not fully recognize the significance of the death of the Rat Man's sister in his guilt and expectations of punishment, the data in the case suggest this enlarged reconstruction and permit further links to be established between the patient's adult neurosis, his transference reactions, and the childhood past. In the Wolf Man, Freud (1918) actually made a highly specific preoedipal reconstruction to 18 months of age; the child's immediate reaction to the primal scene; and long-range, persistent, pathogenic developmental consequences to the shock trauma of the primal scene. At the same time, Freud reconstructed the event backward and forward, wondered whether it was a historical reality or fantasy, a parental or animal primal scene, a primal scene of infancy or of later life, and a shock at the time of the actual event, or a deferred action which first gained traumatic significance at the time of the Wolf Man's famous dream on his fourth birthday. The preoedipal primal scene would then become a phase-specific oedipal trauma (Blum, 1974, 1986). The concept of deferred action maintained the importance of both the event and its unconscious developmental transformation in meaning and influence. Freud pondered these issues in a case which interestingly enough was a return to a theory of pathogenesis largely based upon a single seduction trauma. Questioning the possible role of even phylogenetic memory, Freud vacillated, as he did before and after the Wolf Man case concerning the relative importance of psychic reality and external reality. Implicit in this was also the question of the importance of the reconstruction of historical truth. Later, in constructions in analysis (1937), Freud noted the grain of truth in delusion, and the therapeutic as well as the theoretical necessity of finding the historical truth in which the patient's delusions, screen memories, and fantasies were embedded. In one of his final comments on the centrality of childhood in clinical psychoanalysis, Freud (1939, p. 72) stated that the genesis of a neurosis invariably goes back to early impressions. From the beginnings of psychoanalysis, reconstruction amended, supplemented, organized, and, when necessary, replaced memory and historical legend (Schimek, 1977).

Among the many reasons for the decline of interest in reconstruction was the focus upon the analysis of an idealized transference neurosis as the hallmark of analytic work. "When the transference has risen to this significance, work upon the patient's memories retreats far into the background" (Freud, 1916–1917, p. 444). The ideal intervention was a transference interpretation. The here-and-now seemed much more important, much closer to observation and clinical experience, and much more technically appropriate than the there-and-then of reconstruction. To be sure, analytic experience regularly demonstrated in the patients' associations and behavior, that their character, psychopathology, and personality organization gave indications of fixations and regressions and, in our more recent, enlarged nosology of developmental arrests, inhibitions, and deviations. The transference neurosis, adult neurosis, and infantile neurosis are linked referents in a genetic sequence (Coltrera, 1979).

The analyst acquires a storehouse of information with accumulated evidence of infantile development and disturbance. The transference fantasy itself is after all a modified revision—a recapitulation in the form of a new edition or additions of the childhood past. The transference is living history that is reorganized as it is recovered. The transference fantasy not only depicts a particular self and object representation of the past, such as father or mother, but also a particular set of conflicts during a childhood phase or period of development. Adolescence may reorganize childhood transferences.

Like the archaeologist, the analyst attempts to uncover the buried past, to lift repression, and to make clear that what the patient perceives or misperceives as contemporaneous really belongs to his childhood. At its core, the transference represents childish fantasies and reactions, and transference always has a childish character. To leave the patient only in the realm of a current transference reaction means that the unconscious infantile conflicts of the patient are not interpretatively revealed, and that the patient remains disengaged from the childhood origins of the conflict so that repression remains relatively intact. Transference interpretation should ultimately be genetic, linking the past with the present, however much the past may be continuously reinterpreted in terms of the present. Interpretation should ultimately lead back to the unconscious roots and origins of the transference. In this connection, Glover (1955) stressed this technical necessity: "We are never finished with the transference interpretation until it is finally brought home to roost. To establish the existence of a transference phantasy is only half of our work; it must be detached once more and brought into direct association with infantile life" (p. 152). Reconstruction "makes history," establishing genetic cause and effect and the lifelong reciprocal interrelationship of past and present, fantasy and reality. The separate but interweaving issues of past versus present and of fantasy versus reality have been part of all the controversies associated with reconstruction.

Transference interpretations do have the advantage of great closeness to immediate experience as compared to other forms of extra-analytic interpretation. As powerful and important as transference interpretation is, it is nevertheless not the only form of mutative interpretation, and the extra-analytic sphere is also clinically relevant and significant (Blum, 1980). For Gill (1982) and those identified with this point of view, the here-and-now of the transference remains the essential battlefield of analytic work. The clinical importance of the childhood past fades more or less into limbo. The entire neurosis might be viewed by the analyst as absorbed into the transference. Attempts to lift infantile amnesia and to reconstruct the patient's childhood may be regarded as relatively superfluous. The past is not so much forgotten as lacking in clinical and technical pertinence. The importance of the immediate analyst–analysand relationship and interaction emphasizes the present. This converges with analytic views emphasizing an almost exclusive focus upon psychic reality, but diverges in a paradoxical scrutiny of a two-person analytic field.

An alteration of interest has also taken place in this context with exquisite attention being given to current realities in the analytic situation rather than to the concurrent survey of the patient's contemporary life, past realities, and childhood experience. In these circumstances, neutrality cannot be attained and could not be maintained. The analyst's countertransference, as well as his style, his tendencies to be active or passive, to be questioning, talkative, or silent, to show particular interest in certain types of material such as dreams or fantasies, are given far greater attention than the patient's spontaneous transference patterns and preexisting symptoms and character. Further, transference fantasy could sometimes be viewed more as a reaction to the real analyst and analytic situation than as an edited repetition of the past. The definition of transference may be modified to include new experiences in this neoclassical frame, which is not necessarily a distortion of analytic reality. The extreme of this position is that the only significant reality is that of the analyst and analysand in the psychoanalytic situation.

The patient was, of course, ill prior to coming to analysis, and the role of childhood experiences as well as constitutional factors would be important to the comprehension of pathogenesis and the analysis of unconscious infantile conflicts. As the historical use of reconstruction was sketched (Greenacre, 1980), contemporary attention to countertransference, and who the analyst is as a real person, as well as what he does, are additional factors and determinants of the here-and-now focus (e.g., Freud's age and illness activated fears of object loss in both the Wolfman and H.D.). For those analysts for whom the countertransference is a major guide to the understanding of the transference, it is also a guide to the infantile object relationship; the analysand invites or pressures the analyst to reenact a transference role. Since the patient's past is now filtered not only through the patient's present personality and transference reactions, but also through the analyst's psyche and current countertransference, the patient's infantile past is even further removed from the realities of the analytic situation. The infantile neurosis could only be illuminated through a glass darkly, and the analysis of its derivatives, the reconstruction of its foundations, is then of far more theoretical than clinical interest. Some analysts regard the past as essentially unknowable, and only of hypothetical or theoretical import.

As the historical reality of childhood experience receded from these analytic approaches, questions concerning the plausibility and even the possibility of reconstructing the historical past appeared with renewed intensity. For those analysts who devalued reconstruction, it was now not only not necessary or at least important to recover or reconstruct the long buried experiences of infancy and childhood, but it could be regarded as virtually impossible. A valid, veridical account of the past could not be obtained without the superimposition of biased observations, assumptions, theoretical allegiances, and subjective reinterpretation of the archaic experience. The analytic dialogue is also framed in a particular linguistic and cultural context. Analyst and patient would inevitably rewrite history according to their own proclivities.

Wetzler (1985) noted that the subjectivist, relativist positions of Schafer (1980) and Spence (1982) were partially derived from the ego psychological approach to reconstruction. This approach had been particularly sparked by the work of Kris (1956b), in which earlier events were seen as elaborated into patterns and not authentically recoverable in their original form. With the focus upon defense analysis and the utilization of structural theory, the recovery of actual memories and the reconstruction of discrete experiences were antiquated analytic aims. The past was always viewed through current perspectives, and the linkage of past and present, reestablishing old but severed connections and establishing new connections, seemed far more important than implausible historical reconstructions. Memories themselves, so often fragmentary and distorted, needed to be synthesized into a coherent whole, with its meaning most pertinently connected to the patient's current life and transference situation. In contemporary analysis, reconstruction has supplanted the recovery of distorted childhood memories.

In this view reconstructions are particularly useful in identifying conflicts, explaining the reliance on certain defenses, overcoming resistance, and providing infantile prototypes for the patient's investment in certain areas of childhood experience (Kris Study Group, 1971). Views of the reconstruction of single, remote traumas and of discrete isolated events were radically altered by a number of factors. These factors included the reconstruction of affective and ego states, the importance of extended strain trauma (Kris, 1956c) and cumulative trauma (Khan, 1963), and the realization of the importance of pathogenic object relationships extending across many phases of development and often, throughout preadult life. Remembering became less important than reintegration (Neubauer, 1979). Blum (1980) summarized a more contemporary attitude:

> [I]f the past and present have not been meaningfully interconnected, then in all likelihood the resistance has not been fully overcome, and the basic conflicts have not been subjected to insight and to new ego integration. Reconstruction goes beyond individual memories and fantasies, and is an integrated act [p. 47]; . . .

> [R]econstructive integration identifies patterns and interrelationships rather than isolated conflicts and experiences, and the intrapsychic configurations, consequences, and developmental influences are far more important than actual historical facts. The past is transformed to new

meanings and reorganized on new levels of development [p. 51].

The emergence of ego psychology did not do away with the value of reconstruction, but it brought reconstruction clearly within the dynamic and genetic process of interpretation. "The doctor tries to compel him [the patient] to fit these emotional impulses into the nexus of the treatment and of his life-history" (Freud, 1912, p. 108). Developmental perspectives further increase the complexity of the task of which Freud (1937) asserted: "What we are in search of is a picture of the patient's forgotten years that shall be alike trustworthy and in all essential respects complete" (p. 258). For Freud, the archaeological metaphor, which he used repeatedly in his early case histories, was related to the preservation and analytic resurrection of the archaic world of infantile fantasy and experience. The classical analyst was identified with this view, and Freud's patients were regularly exposed to his office display of archaeological artefacts. His office conveyed the uncovered, buried past. The patients were on a "dig," and the mute objects on the walls and desk and in the cabinets spoke eloquently of the importance of the past, preserved in the present. This forgotten world could be recovered through the lifting of infantile amnesia, and the latent past behind the manifest facade of the present could be rediscovered by making the unconscious conscious. The patient's recovery depended upon discovery, and the preserved past only awaited analytic work to bring it to light.

Freud (1937) later noted that both the archaeologist and the psychoanalyst reconstructed by means of supplementing and combining the surviving remains. This was no longer simple discovery, but the analyst had particular advantages:

The analyst, as we have said, works under more favourable conditions than the archaeologist since he has at his disposal material which can have no counterpart in excavations, such as the repetitions of reactions dating from infancy and all that is indicated by the transference in connection with these repetitions. But in addition to this it must be borne in mind that the excavator is dealing with destroyed objects of which large and important portions have quite certainly been lost, . . . But it is different with the psychical object whose early history the analyst is seeking to recover. . . . All of the essentials are preserved; even things that seem completely forgotten are present somehow and somewhere, and have merely been buried and made inaccessible to the subject. Indeed, it may, as we know, be doubted whether any psychical structure can really be the victim of total destruction. It depends only upon analytic technique whether we shall succeed in bringing what is concealed completely to light [Freud, 1937, pp. 259–260].

These views continue to demonstrate the importance for Freud of memory and of reconstruction, not only of structural conflict but of psychic structure itself. Development was propelled by the endowment in reciprocal interaction with the object world. Infantile object relations and identifications could be reconstructed inside and outside the analytic situation. Reconstruction could also facilitate applied analytic psychobiographical studies. While for Freud psychic structures were alive and immutable, ego psychology later indicated the problems of identifying the most archaic structures because of problems of accretion of subsequent experience and of the even greater problem of developmental transformation. The limitations of the archaeological metaphor and model had to be clarified after Freud's time. Developmental research unimaginable in his day opened new vistas, and raised new questions about pioneer theories of ego development.

Assumptions about memory and perception as passive registrations and inner copies of external events were associated with a model of veridical layering of recorded experience (Schimek, 1975). However, current analytic reconstruction cannot depend on such clear, but obsolete notions. Neither registration, remembering, nor reconstruction reproduces an unaltered artefact, a timeless past newly exposed to the present observers. Rather, past experience is reclaimed with new meanings in a present reorganizing reconstruction.

If developmental transformation was sufficiently far-reaching and complete, it suggested the possibility of discontinuity (Abrams, 1984). The idea of a continuous genetic continuity was now challenged by a genetic–developmental discontinuity which could present formidable obstacles to reconstruction. If the archaic layers of the mind were not likely to be indelibly or perfectly preserved, in any case they were no longer necessarily accessible to the contemporary analyst in their original form. The earliest structures and representations might be irretrievable. There would be rational limits to what could be reconstructed, consistent with developmental knowledge. Furthermore, the actual segment of the experience that was reconstructed would be noted to have important antecedents and significant consequences and ramifications in later development. It was no longer simply a question of reconstructing an infantile trauma with pathogenic consequences, but of reconstructing the vastly overdetermined, mutual influence and sequence of phases of development, ego functions, object relations, and their effect on character formation. What was reconstructed was not simple, pathogenic, actual events but the child's complex interpretation of his experience, and his reaction to it, taking his endowment into account (Weil, 1970). The meaning attached to traumatic experience, for example, of the primal scene, was far more than overstimulation generally injurious to development, but importantly included the child's misinterpretation of the primal scene as a sadomasochistic assault. The unconscious fantasy elaboration and the structural and developmental impact of a particular experience or set of experiences, became more important than the actual history. The telescoping of memory (A. Freud, 1951) and the problems of accretion and stratification added to the complexity of the task of reconstruction. Freud had early on wrestled with these problems, and on December 6, 1896 wrote to Fliess, "our psychic mechanism has come into being by a process of stratification: the material present in the form of memory traces being subjected from time to time to a *rearrangement* in accordance with fresh circumstances—to a *retranscription*" (Masson, 1985, p. 207). This was related to Freud's later reflection (1937):

> One of the most ticklish problems that confronts the archaeologist is notoriously the determination of the relative age of his finds; and if an object makes its appearance in some particular level, it often remains to be decided whether it belongs to that level or whether it was carried down to that level owing to some subsequent disturbance. It is easy to imagine the corresponding doubts that arise in the case of analytic constructions [p. 259].

To acknowledge scientific skepticism and complexity, however, was not to acknowledge that all interpretation and reconstruction were to be doubted. In psychoanalysis, "hermeneutics," dispensed with genetic cause and later effect, and challenged traditional attitudes toward psychoanalytic epistemology. Those analysts who adopted hermeneutics questioned psychoanalysis as a natural observational science. Psychoanalysis was concerned with meaning, and latent meanings were variable, nonobjective, and not subject to natural science verification. Outside of psychoanalysis, the new criticism of historical reconstruction was also related to a relativist shift in science, particularly in quantum physics, from determinism into probability. The uncertainty principle was to prevail, and the observer inevitably influenced what was observed. There could be no objective, context-free observation, no avoidance of preestablished orientation, and thus no objectivity about historical actuality. Reconstruction compounded the bias of observation. Facts could no longer verifiably speak for themselves, but were subject to multiple narratives and subjectively assigned meanings in an evolving psychoanalytic dialogue (Schafer, 1980). The narrative aspect of psychoanalysis is not a substitute for historical truth, but is presumed to be the form in which history exists. These propositions sharpen scientific skepticism and analytic self-scrutiny; at the same time "preferred explanatory story lines" imply doubt and disbelief concerning the reliability and validity of genetic interpretation and reconstruction. Here the contemporary two-person model of the psychoanalytic process does not lead to refined and more accurate reconstruction, but to intuitive construction.

Related to these viewpoints, all memories are partially shaped in the present, and are to be regarded as screen memories and transference phenomena. References to the past are disguised compromise formations which could only be fully understood in the here-and-now of the present. The past is "reinvented and recreated" in the context of the present. Hence, the past is not only not reconstructed in analysis, it cannot be objectively reconstructed since there are multiple probable realities. Personal history thus becomes a "story line" with its own coherence and internal consistency, but an autobiography written with a great deal of poetic license. Analyst and patient incorporate varying degrees of fiction and take their own liberties with fact which, in any case, cannot be fully ascertained. Narrative appeal, intelligibility, consistency, and coherence virtually obliterate the question of correspondence with factual history. For analysts with these views reconstruction is our impossible dream.

Spence (1982) dismisses the notion that there is any possible veridical picture of the past and regards any analytic interpretation as true only in its own analytic space. Clinical material does not exist independently of the observer, and language itself so alters and transforms perceptual experience that analytic work would paradoxically oppose accurate reconstruction. The analyst superimposes his own theoretical preconceptions and his own bias in the selection and organization of the data of observation. There is no shared objectivity or reality, and all meaning presumes construction. For Spence (1987) this precludes an accurate search for historical truth. What is called the past becomes part of an analytic mythopoesis, a pseudoscientific account of a person's life history. The so-called Freudian metaphor tempts the analyst (in this view) to believe that he can uncover the infantile contents of the dynamic unconscious and the historical truth concerning key happenings in the patient's past. What is fact, and how facts are arranged, is subjectively determined. Further, the analyst might narcissistically impose his construction or submit to the patient's construction. History is not recalled or reconstructed, but is cocreated as an analytic legend within a shared belief system. Infantile life was long ago and far away, and infantile wishes and defenses might not be recognized and regarded as "experience near."

If taken to its outer limit, this point of view goes further than the formulation that there is no analytic reconstruction, only hypothetical construction. At its limit, for Freudians who hold to the importance of childhood and its reconstructions, it is tantamount to a reduction and devaluation of the importance of childhood. The regular clinical analytic encounter with the child and the childishness in the patient leads patient and analyst to the past.

It is then not possible to accept that there is no factual correspondence to any reconstruction of the childhood past, only internal coherence, and no external reality, only psychic reality. Rather, the analyst is compelled to search for the truth in the delusion and the relationship of fantasy and reality. Analysts identified with this view will attempt to reconstruct psychic and external realities; the patient's inner experience, and its essential meaning and consequences in terms of developmental phase, preexisting and subsequent intrapsychic conflict and fantasy, and pathogenic influence. A patient who has been reared by a psychotic parent must first be able to reconstruct childhood psychic reality, object relations, and crucial identifications before being able to understand fears of going and being crazy, or of driving the analyst crazy; the terror of regression and disorganization; the deep distrust of the analyst's thinking. The transference paradigm in which the analyst or the patient represents the psychotic parent, reciprocally illuminates reconstruction of the patient's childhood as it was unconsciously experienced and intrapsychically interpreted. The patient's mode of experience, his fantasy life, and fantasies about his life, are reconstructed in the shared and shifting perspectives of analytic work.

Contemporary analysts who espouse reconstruction and its continuing therapeutic and theoretical importance hardly regard themselves as being axiomatic or dogmatic. Multiple perspectives and "truths" do not preclude any appreciation of actual and inferred realities. Here there is theoretical disagreement with the notion of narrative truth. The choice among alternative reconstructions is left enigmatic in Schafer's (1983) proposition, "There are numerous, perhaps countless, mental models of any one analysand that may be constructed, all more or less justified by 'data' " (p. 40). I do not believe that Spence and analysts who dispense with reconstruction are insisting that all historical accounts are equally coherent, plausible, valid, or useful. But this approach would leave analyst and patient in doubt, for example, about reality, authenticity, and causality. Any consensually valid or seemingly verifiable interpretation or reconstruction would be regarded as illusion. Neither patient nor analyst could acquire a sense of scientific conviction as opposed to a type of religious conviction or shared illusion. Analyst and patient would explicitly or implicitly have a sense of elusive, ever-shifting reality far beyond the usual view that the past inevitably looks somewhat different in different phases of analysis and in different phases of life. The subjectivist view does not preclude that the analyst rediscovers already established and confirmed experiences, but it is the meanings of these experiences which remain so fluid and subjective. In itself, subjectivism provides a useful argument against dogmatism, and against the concretization of metaphor. However, the implied radical relativity of reconstruction and multiplicity of clinical models, could substitute a dubious pluralism for dogmatism. Open mindedness and tolerance for ambiguity should not become the endorsement of narrative composition in analysis.

Contemporary psychoanalysis does not lean upon familial confirmation of childhood reconstructions as in the pioneer days. But neither does it presuppose that an individual's authentic life history is not unalterably and profoundly important. Though perception and the sense of reality are immediately colored by fantasy and condensed with it, and experience is subjective, the facts of life do not disappear in attempted and approximate reconstruction. The importance of psychic determinism is inextricably related to the discovery of genetic–developmental sequence, and the importance of all of childhood for the understanding of the adult personality. Coherence alone might have no more closeness to actual experience than the coherence achieved by the secondary elaboration of the dream. Without such secondary elaboration, the irrational dream might appear to be totally unintelligible. But this coherence may be quite misleading without an understanding of the structure of the dream and the disguised form in which the latent content of the dream appears in the manifest content.

Freud, the empirical scientist, believed in a pragmatic scientific truth that was not subjective fantasy. Psychoanalysis was based upon "love of truth" and was in possession of the "truth," and Freud would, in all probability, not have found the propositions of "narrative truth" convincing or congenial. For Freud, in apparent divergence from Spence (1982), psychoanalytic truth was based upon correspondence with facts. Freud (1914c, p. 77) averred that psychoanalysis was a science whose foundations were therefore based upon observation alone. There was truth, and there was delusion, an external reality, and a historical actuality. An external or pragmatic material reality could be understood apart from the patient's irrational and infantile psychic reality. Material and external reality were essentially synonymous but not carefully defined in relation to the actual past and "historic truth." Freud (1939) contrasted the external world and its psychic representatives from psychic reality:

All these phenomena, the symptoms as well as the restrictions on the ego and the stable character-changes, have a *compulsive* quality: that is to say that they have great psychical intensity and at the same time exhibit a far-reaching independence of the organization of the other mental processes, which are adjusted to the demands of the real external world and obey the laws of logical thinking. They [the pathological phenomena] are insufficiently or not at all influenced by external reality, pay no attention to it or to its psychical representatives, so that they may easily come into active opposition to both of them. They are, one might say, a State within a State, an inaccessible party, with which co-operation is impossible, but which may succeed in over-coming what is known as the normal party and forcing it into its service. If this happens, it implies a domination by an internal psychical reality over the reality of the external world and the path to a psychosis lies open [p. 76].

Having wrestled with the problem of the differentiation of personal myth from actual experience, neither Freud nor those analysts identified with the genetic point of view upon which reconstruction is based would disengage from reality–fantasy issues in psychoanalytic work. Freud (1933) observed, "If what we believe were really a matter of indifference, if there were no such thing as knowledge distinguished among our opinions by corresponding to reality, we might build bridges just as well out of cardboard as out of stone, we might inject our patients with a decagram of morphine instead of a centigram, and might use tear-gas as a narcotic instead of ether" (p. 176).

Freud (1933) also asserted, "This correspondence with the real external world we call 'truth'. It remains the aim of scientific work even if we leave the practical value of that work out of account" (p. 170). This did not imply belief in an absolute truth, or an absence of scientific skepticism. Freud (1940) preserved a balanced awareness of the limitations of the psychic apparatus and human capacity to test and understand reality, stating, "Reality will always remain 'unknowable'" (p. 196).

It is true that the analyst listens and responds, undoubtedly influenced by his previous analytic education and experience. The analytic data themselves are influenced by the analyst's own input and his theoretical and subjective interests and resistances. Every analytic situation does have its own unique realities which need to be defined, as in the case of the analytic training situation and analysis conducted under the auspices of a psychoanalytic institute. Despite subjective assumptions and preferences, it is impressive how much of a patient's conflicts and experiences may be understood by different analysts in terms of commonalities. I am not referring here to analysts who start out with the theoretical preconceptions and preferences of an alternate school of psychoanalysis. The plethora of evidence provided from the analytic data obtained will point in particular directions and tend to converge in forms which eliminate many alternative possibilities. Depression due to divorce may be associated with the revival of trauma associated with childhood object loss; for example, the separation from or death of a parent. The death may be associated with unresolved oedipal guilt, incomplete mourning, and fantasies about resurrection and reunion. Denial of the early loss may be related to later denial of serious disturbances that lead to the breakup of the marriage, with fantasies of reconciliation defending against feelings of betrayal and desertion. The traumatic experience of the death of a parent in childhood is not simply revived in the transference pattern. All traumatic experiences are associated with ego regression, disorganization, and confusion, compounded by denial and other defenses. In this connection, anniversary reactions are symptomatic constructions. Fantasy and reality have to be ordered and reorganized, within a genetic-developmental framework.

The restoration of cause and effect and cohesion of the personality depend upon transference analysis in the here-and-now, but also upon reconstruction of the past which approximates as closely as is possible to the conscious and unconscious meaning of the child's actual experience. This gives a genetic frame for the crucial analysis of the pathogenic unconscious conflicts and fantasies. The denial of reality, for example, in the case of the childhood death of a loved one, with ensuing guilt and self-reproach, and the effect of that loss upon the surviving parent and siblings, will be crucial for understanding the developmental impact of the loss. How can the analytic revival of unconscious conflict and trauma, grief and mourning, be understood without reconstruction? In contemporary psychoanalysis, the patient's history is completed, corrected, and also created with reorganization of the personality. The past is rediscovered, as in early psychoanalysis, but it also takes on elaborate new meanings which did not exist in childhood. The ego confusion of the child is progressively clarified in analysis, and the conscious understanding of far more advanced levels of integration would not have been available to the child without treatment and further maturation. Childhood experience and meanings are therefore variously retrieved and recovered but also reconstructed and recreated (Blum, 1983). In this process, the facts are scrutinized from fresh perspectives and processed with an understanding enormously enriched by analytic insight. This analytic reexamination of personal history has been designated a "second look" (Novey, 1968). It is actually childhood regularly revisited, an ongoing series of reexaminations and new scrutiny which places fantasy and facts in a new light, contributing to analysis as a "second chance." There is a continuous interplay of external and internal reality and reciprocal effects of external and internal reality on each other. In the case of childhood intrapsychic identification with an external object, it alters internal reality, external object relationship, and in turn external reality adaptation. The appreciation of external–internal interaction becomes part of the process of genetic interpretation and reconstruction, and the analysis of unconscious intrapsychic conflict. An exclusive focus upon psychic reality would be a reductionist parody of the psychoanalytic process, though the "intrapsychic" remains the hallmark of analytic orientation. Psychic reality and external reality are different, yet interrelated domains with mutual influence. Noting that fantasy and reality each have a share among the essential elements of neurosis, Freud (1916–1917) stated, "Here we simply have once again one of the complemental relations that I have so often mentioned; moreover it is the strangest of all we have met with" (p. 370).

Beyond the coordination of the patient's fantasies with his real experience is an appreciation of multiple realities and the role of a child's developmental phase, family, culture, and education. Reconstruction may take into account the role of shared fantasy, the child's enactment of unconscious fantasies of the parent, the types of responses the child elicits from the parent, and the appreciation by the child of the parents' relationship and their conflicts and concerns. The analytic process will tend to stimulate the patient to explore his past, and consciously or unconsciously to engage in reconstruction. The patient can then safely reexperience the mode and content of disavowed infantile thought, feeling, conflict and fantasy. Unconscious conflict and fantasy are genetically interpreted in the overall context of the patient's reconstructed childhood.

Many patients find themselves talking to relatives about their childhood, attending to old photographs or home movies, recovering mementos of childhood, visiting old homes and cemeteries, unearthing diaries and letters of long ago. These activities all have transference meaning, as does reconstruction proper. One cannot, however, literally and concretely "go home again" in regression or reconstruction to a transformed past.

Our case histories are not myths, and patients have authentic real families with their own unique life history. If the analyst doubts his own interpretations and reconstructions, the patient will lack conviction about the analysis or authenticity about his life. Such disbelief can undermine analytic inferences which are "beyond reasonable doubt." An elegantly written case history may read like a novel but contain and utilize historical facts which are not only given meaning in themselves, but lend meaning to the patient's life. The renovation and remodeling of the personality partially depend upon the analytic reorganization of the patient's life history (Greenacre, 1975). It is necessary to understand not only significant events but also how these events were endowed with additional meaning at different phases of life. The limits of reconstruction, and especially of early preoedipal reconstruction, have to be kept in mind, especially in regard to reconstruction of preverbal issues.

Reconstruction is always an approximation with the explanatory fit consistent with known developmental knowledge; for example, when a child is capable of representational thought and/or experiencing self-criticism and guilt. Fantasy and memory may be disguised versions of each other but actual experience continues to be important (Sachs, 1967; Wetzler, 1985). There are significant differences between universal fantasy and actual experience, such as between primal scene fantasy and actual exposure or between fantasied desertion and actual object loss. Though they are not easily distinguished, they have different developmental and clinical consequences (Greenacre, 1956, 1975; Blum, 1980). What is or becomes traumatic may be related to the validation of an unconscious fantasy and is elaborated in fantasy. Real object loss may elicit far more anxiety and guilt than fantasied desertion, and traumatic experience will be associated with obligatory tendencies toward both regression and reenactment.

Reconstruction remains important for clinical analysis and theory formation (Ekstein and Rangell, 1961). General theoretical propositions such as the concept of psychic trauma or the sequence and overlap of developmental phase may be independently reconstructed in a specific psychoanalytic case. At the same time, reconstruction may involve cautious extension from general psychoanalytic and developmental knowledge. The integration of analytic and developmental studies promises deeper, more accurate, and more comprehensive reconstruction.

Based upon logical inference from newly available clinical evidence reconstruction may pose new hypotheses or questions. This would apply, for example, to the reconstruction of protracted, massive trauma and its sequelae in Holocaust survivors and their children. What the parents deny and forget, the children "remember," and construct in fantasy (Kestenberg, 1972). The process of reconstruction tends to extend the domain of the ego while facilitating the analytic process. There should be greater access to what was previously unconscious and greater clarity about what was previously confused and distorted. The analytic result should be new self-knowledge, new options, and mature relationships (Frank, 1990). Reconstruction makes a decisive difference in clinical analysis and is mutative. The past within the present is transformed forging a new vision of reality.

Chapter Eight

The Therapeutic Value and Validity of Reconstruction in Clinical Psychoanalysis

> The correct reconstruction, you must know, of such forgotten experiences of childhood always has a great therapeutic effect, whether they permit of objective confirmation or not [Freud, 1926b, p. 216].

Reconstruction evolved with the development of psychoanalysis as a method of treatment and as a science of unconscious mental processes, which, along with unconscious contents, were shown to be related to childhood and infantile life. Correlating the origins of psychoanalysis with the recapture of the childhood past, Freud (1913) stated: "it [psychoanalysis] began by discovering the genesis of neurotic symptoms, and was led, as time went on, to turn its attention to other psychical structures and to construct a genetic psychology which would apply to them too" (p. 183). "Psycho-analysis has brought to light the wishes, the thought-structures and the developmental processes of childhood" (p. 189).

The "genesis of a neurosis invariably goes back to very early impressions . . ." (p. 73). Freud goes on to say in a footnote, "This, therefore, makes it nonsensical to say that one is practising psycho-analysis if one excludes from examination and consideration precisely those early periods—as happens in some quarters" (Freud, 1939, n1, p. 73). A historical here-and-now approach would not be psychoanalysis any more than would an exclusive focus on the patient's external life or past history. Freud did not abandon the clinical or theoretical importance of reconstruction; indeed, he emphasized its importance in his final papers. Freud also conveyed this interest in reconstruction through the analytic setting of his office. The patient who entered Freud's office was not in a neutral setting. He was exposed to archaeological artifacts as though in a museum. A picture of ancient Egypt at Abu Simbel with its giant statues of Ramses, hung over the couch. The patient was invited to an "archaeological dig" into the past; for example, Freud immediately informed the poet H.D. that they were meeting in the childhood of man. The task of psychoanalysis was to reconstruct the patient's forgotten childhood from the traces left behind, "What we are in search of is a picture of the patient's forgotten years that shall be alike trustworthy and in all essential respects complete" (Freud, 1937, p. 258).

Reconstruction, so formulated, is both a goal of analysis and a technique toward achieving the goal. The analysts in our group concurred with Greenacre (1975, 1981) that reconstruction was a cornerstone of psychoanalysis. There were, however, differences of opinion concerning the relative therapeutic value of reconstruction in comparison with the mutative effect of transference interpretation and current extratransference interpretation. The analytic task of reconstruction can only be accomplished by work with the patient in the present here-and-now of the analytic situation and the transference. It begins with the analyst's own initial intrapsychic constructions, hypotheses about the patient's life history, pathogenesis, sources of ego strength and weakness (Greenacre, 1975). The analyst listens and learns and develops tentative constructions about the patient's life and problems. Associations begin to form a network of connections, converging in an emerging picture of some significant aspect of the patient's childhood; for example, the consequences of a severe illness, the divorce of parents, the role of servants as surrogate parents. The defensive constellations of childhood are noted, especially as they function as resistance in the analytic process. The analytic process opens pathways between the past and present. The analyst gradually understands how the individual of today developed from the infant and child that he once was and in some respects continues to be. The patient learns that who he is and what disturbs him are linked to who he has been. What might have been an effective defense or adaptation in childhood may long ago have outlived its usefulness, though it is still present in adult life.

The patient cannot relinquish the unconsciously determined childish pattern, which is related to the patient's symptomatic and personality disturbance. From the memories and screen memories, the transference, dreams, and fantasies, the flow of ideas and affective responses, the analyst charts genetic–developmental trends. The analyst's construction is already a cocomposition because it is in part suggested and composed by the patient's communications. The data will strongly recommend one specific reconstruction among many less "fitting" alternatives. This will become the reconstruction that is proposed as a technical intervention, to organize the patient's internal and external experience, and rewrite aspects of the patient's autobiography that is being relived in the transference and in neurotic repetitions. Why was a patient having so much difficulty with her son? Why did she hide her own treatment from her parents and sneak past them to her analytic hour? Why was she so full of self-reproach and ready to provoke her husband and son when she visited or failed to visit her parents? Was not her tendency to plead and protest, punish and be punished related to her being a very seductive, demanding little girl, as well as an oversensitive "crybaby," crushed by the slightest disapproval or disappointment? Reconstruction will take into account drive and disposition, innate endowment, as well as maturation and development. The vicissitudes of life and not just of the drives are followed. The actual personalities of parents and siblings; parental responses to the child's pleas and protests; parental expectations and values; school and peer pressures (e.g., the influence of strict, parochial school education) will all be reconstructed.

At some point, depending on tact and timing, the patient's overall readiness, and the potential contribution to the analytic process, the analyst offers his refined construction to the patient as a reconstruction.

> We avoid telling him at once things that we have often discovered at an early stage, and we avoid telling him the whole of what we think we have discovered. We reflect carefully over when we shall impart the knowledge of one of our constructions to him and we wait for what seems to us the suitable moment—which it is not always easy to decide. As a rule we put off telling him of a construction or explanation till he himself has so nearly arrived at it that only a single step remains to be taken, though that step is in fact the decisive synthesis [Freud, 1940, p. 178].

The reconstruction is now a direct intervention, an overt, verbalized communication in the analytic process. The patient may disagree, may resist a particularly objectionable aspect of the reconstruction, or may treat the reconstruction with disdain or indifference. Conversely, the reconstruction may help to resolve resistance, it may be welcome and add to feeling understood and acquiring understanding, it may spur additional transference reactions of gratitude or guilt. Usually, the reconstruction will facilitate the emergence of new material and the further elaboration of the patient's conflicts and fantasies. The reconstruction is drawn into the transference and analytic work where it will be tested, revised, and where it becomes a model for further genetic interpretation and reconstruction. The recent past and isolated areas of contemporary life will also be drawn into the process of reconstruction—downward and upward.

The reconstruction of contemporary life is often necessary in adult analysis. Although this is not what is generally meant by reconstruction as a clinical and theoretical process applied to the childhood past, a patient's contemporary life may also be rather obscure. The patient's dysfunction at school or at work and problems in a marriage may be greatly in need of clarification. The onset of an illness may be described as insidious or inexplicable by a patient, and the regressive confusion and misunderstanding need to be clarified and coherently organized. Collusive secrets may emerge only when the present-day collusion is subject to analytic examination along with its past connections, and sometimes hidden motives for treatment.

The onset of a personality regression or an outbreak of symptoms may be disconnected from its actual psychological context, and the reasons for or meanings of the symptoms are subject to secondary elaboration and rationalization. A successful executive believed that his insomnia was caused by competitive pressures in the marketplace so that he stayed up at night preoccupied with "beating the competition." He was indirectly correct in that the insomnia resulted from unconscious oedipal rivalry. The rivals he admired and feared most were not in the marketplace but in his own family. The outbreak of insomnia followed the attainment of executive authority when a father figure abdicated the chief executive post upon retirement. The patient's insomnia was related to guilt over an unconscious oedipal victory. He could not allow himself to enjoy his work or his wife since he had unconsciously fantasied that he had taken his father's power, penis, and wife for himself. His insomnia was not only a result of his seeking to be a successful competitor but of his being "wrecked by success," guilty, and fearful of retaliation by his vanquished rival. The outbreak of an adult neurosis will be illuminated by the analytic work which will ultimately lead to the reconstruction of the infantile neurosis. In the case just cited, for example, the linking of the adult insomnia to unconscious infantile conflicts associated with early childhood nightmares, sleep disturbance, and tics would demonstrate the reconstructive linking of present and past with reciprocal illumination and clarification.

In child analysis, the clarification of the child's present-day life, and his or her family and school situation are a very important part of analytic work from the surface. Parents infrequently give a distorted picture of their own attitudes and behaviors with the child, and there may be significant distortions or omissions concerning the child's life. The confusion is compounded by the child's ego immaturity and defenses, so that much needs to be learned about the child's current life. The child very much lives in the present and may not be motivated or readily able to forge links with the past. The child has little grasp of his life situation or any understanding that what he plays out with the child analyst may repeat the conflicts and struggles that have occurred at home or repeat derivatives of past traumas. The parents may report a child's poor school performance, but may minimize or not recognize their criticism and devaluation of the child and the hostility associated with their compensatory teaching, tutoring, and bribing the child to study. The child's treatment itself may take on the meaning of tutoring, with success to be measured with the child's school performance and grades. Again, clarification of the child's current conflicts and their association with the parents' narcissistic ambitions for the child and their competitive pressures will be preliminary to reconstruction of the child's infantile conflicts. This clarification would precede

establishing the connecting links between the child's earlier life and the present childhood disorder. What has
been called "reconstruction upwards" is also related to
working from the surface, interpreting what is more accessible before what is more remote, and interpreting defense before contents. It must also be kept in mind that
the past may defend against the present just as the present
may defend against the past. A too rapid leap into the past
may only intensify resistance, add to confusion concerning
fantasy elaboration of experience, and complicate later
efforts at more careful and tactful reconstruction.

The childhood past which is reconstructed is both
retrieved and recreated in analytic work. The child's fantasied distortions and elaborations of his experience are
reconstructed with an attempt to understand the child's
own selection, synthesis, and mythopoesis. The veridical,
historical past is also reconstructed as it is pertinent to the
analytic process and permitted by it. The next step is a
new integration of fantasy and reality which may be considered to be a more complete reconstruction or an outcome or product of reconstruction.

In a further integration, the reconstruction will be
connected to later development and the present. What the
reconstruction then accomplishes is not a recapitulation
or reexperience; it is not the past as it was or as it was
experienced by the child, but a new integration on an
adult developmental level. Self and object representations
are transformed and become more realistic. The analytic
dialogue transforms both past and present as the patient's
life is reexperienced and experienced differently. This is
not a static past, analogous to an archaeological relic, but
a dynamic remodeling which continues within and contributes to the analytic process. Pathological personality distortions were acquired mainly during childhood, although
the pathological influences of adolescence and adulthood
could in addition be of momentous or minor significance.

Reconstruction involves psychic and external reality in continuous interaction and is neither an id psychology of unconscious fantasy in a vacuum, nor an environmental set of uninterpreted, historical events. Reconstruction leads to a more comprehensive understanding of individual development and promotes the integration of dissociated fragments of external experience and the inner world. These fragments prove to be dynamically and developmentally patterned or interrelated.

The analyst will also be currently aware that simple genetic continuities are unlikely, that adult anxiety dreams and phobic avoidance are derivative only in degree (e.g., of childhood typhoid fever and subsequent nightmares). In contemporary psychoanalysis, developmental considerations and clinical experience affirm that the infantile, adult, and transference neurosis are not identical. The adult neurosis is not a replica of the infantile neurosis, but a transformed, edited derivative.

Contemporary reconstruction is far more sophisticated than the reconstruction of the pioneer days. It is a far more complex process than suggested by the archaeological metaphor with its many references to the inert and the inanimate. The analyst has the advantage and the burden of a live patient and a living history. In addition to its specific content, reconstruction establishes a genetic template and a frame of reference for interpretation, with intersecting vistas and perspectives. The process of reconstruction is intrinsically related to the process of interpretation and is both a foundation and overarching dimension of genetic interpretation. Allied with genetic interpretation and alloyed to it, reconstruction facilitates psychic change through verbalized conscious insight and expanding ego domination of conflicts, fantasies, affects, and acting-out tendencies. The personal, subjective, transformed significance of historical experience is understood anew in the context of the analytic work.

Though criticized as mere conjecture or as intellectualized efforts to suggest, educate, or indoctrinate, reconstruction proceeds from analytic work. It aims at a corrective, cognitive, and emotional experience which leads to a rationally based conviction for both analytic partners about the unique, authentic, inevitably idiosyncratic past and pathogenesis. It should be noted that a reconstructive orientation is a clinical application of the genetic point of view. It is a search for antecedent cause, connection, and influence for understanding the roots of the personality and the neurosis. The past lives in the analytic situation and informs the analytic context and evolving life history. Reconstruction ultimately provides the framework for transference and genetic interpretation so that transference interpretation and reconstruction are interactive and complementary.

Free association tends to drift downward toward derivatives of the unconscious and temporally backwards toward the experiences and reactions of childhood. Free association will become patterned in relation to a transference fantasy or paradigm, and this pattern will be traced to its historical antecedents in the infantile neurosis and childhood. Past or present may defend against the other, blend with the other, and represent autobiographical constructions (Kris, 1956b). From a technical viewpoint, as previously indicated, it is the present that usually must be addressed first. Currently active thoughts and feelings that are preconscious are amalgamated with the past, which is simultaneously revived and dramatized in the transference in the analytic situation (Kanzer, 1953). Past and present converge and may point to the future. The rapid and very early reconstructions of the pioneer days have been superseded by careful systematic analysis of transference and resistance, and by very careful attention to the cumulative anamnesis derived from the patient's analytic history and free association. This is necessary in order for the patient to have a sense of the pathogenic significance of his infantile living and reliving and persisting conflicts: "we must treat his illness, not as an event of the past, but as a present-day force . . . we have to do our therapeutic work on it [the transference], which consists in a large measure in tracing it back to the past" (Freud, 1914b, pp. 151–152).

While within the group, as among psychoanalysts in general, there was some difference of opinion on the timing and emphasis of interpretation of the present versus interpretation of the past (the here-and-now versus the there-and-then), and these polarized tendencies were found within individual analysts. Past and present are in a dynamic relationship, defined and interpreted by each other. The patient presents his subjective versions of the past, his screen memories, constructions, personal myths, and a defensively edited and revised autobiography. The past could be represented in the present, but the present could also be represented in the past, with past, present, and intended future exerting a mutual influence upon their meaning and representation. The past is, initially and in degree, a contemporary construction selectively organized in the present. And both past and present acquire different meanings in different phases of life and in different phases of psychoanalysis. Temporal and causal sequence are reorganized, and historical facts and configurations are structured in terms of causality and historical contexts (Friedman, 1983). As the childhood roots of neurosis are reconstructed, resistances are loosened and analyzed. This permits correction of memory fragments, distortions, and screens, the lifting of areas of amnesia, and the clarification of regressive alteration and confusion. When reconstruction has functioned as a command to remember, what follows are usually screen memories

(Reider, 1953) requiring dynamic clarification, transference interpretation, and genetic reconstruction. Reconstruction fills in the blanks and bridges psychic and external reality. In contemporary analysis, reconstruction, combined with transference analysis, has supplanted the recovery of memories in theory and practice.

Reconstruction is essentially related to genetic interpretation. It is, in essence, an explanatory proposition: at a particular time and developmental phase this and that must have happened, and you must have reacted in this way, and that is why you now, under these conditions and circumstances, react in this way and with that consequence. The explanatory concept refers both to real experience and to the history and evolution of interrelated fantasy. As an explanatory concept, reconstruction paradoxically provides access to new material and subsequent explanations that could not yet be formulated in childhood. For example, reconstruction may be utilized to establish the history of such defenses as denial following object loss in early childhood and the developmental and pathogenic influence of inconsistent identifications with different objects in childhood and adolescence (Faimberg and Corel, 1990).

The facilitating effect and progressive thrust of reconstruction, counterposed to its role in the completion and reorganization of memory, was noted by Freud (1937): "for the archaeologist the reconstruction is the aim and end of his endeavours while for analysis the construction is only a preliminary labour" (p. 260). Reconstruction clarifies what has only been vaguely understood; for example, when infantile confusion persists concerning a parent's depression and emotional unavailability. This reconstruction is then tied to the patient's own depressive tendencies and to feelings that the analyst, representing the depressed parent, is not listening or interested.

Not only are past and present reorganized, but new meanings are given to a whole set of experiences and reactions. These meanings did not exist in the same way as before so that psychic representations are remodeled even as new meaning is created. Reconstruction makes sense of inchoate ideas and ineffable, affect-laden experience. What could not be put into words by the young child concerning the child's own or his parents' hospitalization is verbally organized and articulated in the reconstruction. The child's denial contributed to a disturbed sense of reality, cognitive confusion, and ego constriction. Affects which also could not be verbalized such as the feelings of helplessness, panic, and rage are differentiated, expressed, and reexperienced with the comprehension afforded by the reconstruction. A lifelike sculpture is not "liberated" from the marble but reassembled and modeled in the process of reconstruction. Thus, reconstruction leads to recovery through discovery, but also through the created and creative attainment of meaning and insight which did not and could not exist in that form in the past (Blum, 1983). The "facts of life" are revised and elaborated, altered in their intrapsychic meaning and analytic significance. Reconstruction promotes new ego integration on higher levels of development through the deeper analysis of unconscious conflict and trauma.

The revival of interest in reconstruction and the importance accorded to it as a cornerstone of psychoanalysis have occurred in conjunction with a reexamination of psychic trauma and of fantasy. Despite the fact that the events of the past can never be exactly known and that it is the intrapsychic assimilation, meaning, and consequences of past experience that are of fundamental importance, the necessity of reconstruction in clinical psychoanalysis was apparent. The compelling significance of reconstruction for both patient and analyst was repeatedly affirmed and emphasized. Though all childhood experience is ego edited and subjectively misinterpreted, the value of reconstruction also lies in its role of clarifying what was obscure, distorted, and forgotten in childhood: what was confused as a result of ego immaturity, defense, regression, and wishful thinking, the effects of psychic trauma, developmental imbalance, deficit, or deviation. Even when a patient is very much aware of such an important event as the death of his father in childhood, this particular traumatic situation has many unconscious ramifications. Kris (1956c) doubted the possibility of reconstructing and recovering real traumatic experiences from childhood because they become molded into complex, transformed patterns. These patterns absorb and supersede the specific events (Kris Study Group, 1971, p. 125). Kris was critical of simple reconstructions and acknowledged that one of the major tasks of reconstruction and of analysis, in general, was to identify pathological patterns and restore the links between past and present. The shock trauma of the dramatic single event gave way to cumulative trauma and strain trauma, and to noxious, pathogenic development.

While Freud, at various times, shifted positions concerning the significance of fantasy and real experience, analysts in the main, accepted Freud's views on the importance of the reconstruction of traumatic experiences. The majority also concurred with the importance of pattern, but felt that discrete, unconscious, traumatic situations and conflicts could often be reconstructed, taking into account the telescoping of cumulative and strain trauma.

The two poles in the field were that reconstruction was imperative in clinical psychoanalysis and that reconstruction was impossible in clinical psychoanalysis. The latter view dispensed with the importance of historical fact and was prologue to the current popularity of "narrative truth." Reconstruction was then associated with a one-sided concern with an ostensibly factual reality, and with the notion that "questions about historical truths are either impossible to answer . . . or relatively unimportant" (Spence, 1982, p. 276).

Reconstruction remains essential for the vast majority of analysts following Freud, in terms of the real experience of patients, their families, and their unique life history with its own fabric of "happenings," meanings, and personal and familial myths. The patient who had a daydream of a massacre of his present family did not directly relate this to the death of his father in childhood and to his fear of reexperiencing death in the family. The analysis of the many layers of meaning in the daydream involves not only the fantasy of parricide but its validation in his father's death. The daydream also revealed identification with the patient's mother's reactions to his father's death and contributed to the reconstruction of his mother's reaction to the massacre of her family of origin in the Holocaust. The same conflicts were discerned in the patient's transference and screen memories.

Because of condensation and displacement, regressive alteration and developmental transformation, the transference cannot recapitulate the development of either the infantile neurosis or the adult neurosis. To put this another way, the transference is not a simple repetition of the past but a defensively distorted fantasy version of the past revived in the present and interpenetrating with the present. Although transference is a resistance to remembering, it is also a living history and a form of remembering what has been forgotten and repressed. The unconscious conflicts and traumas of childhood are repeated in the transference fantasy in an edited compromise formation. Thus, although transference is a major source, it is never the only source of the data and evidence on which reconstruction is based. It is the transference that is also paradoxically the main target of reconstruction. If the latter is simply based upon transference phenomena alone it will be suggestive and speculative (Arlow, 1991).

The analytically inferred past is integrated into valid and convincing explanatory approximations. Ultimately, reconstructions are necessary antidotes for transference resistances (Frank, 1990) and explanations of transference repetition. Since acting out of transference serves resistance through repeating the past, reconstruction promotes the analytic resolution of acting out. The complementary processes of interpretation and reconstruction tend to break the cycle of repetition compulsion and the patterns of relating and reacting that are embedded in an unrecognized reliving of the past. Though reconstruction may be at a greater degree of abstraction and further removed from the immediate analytic experience, it is also directly tied to the patient's childhood experience. Reconstruction is childhood revisited, reviewed, and then recreated and remodeled. The patient has a second look (Novey, 1968) and a new opportunity to examine the child he was and is, the child that still lives in the adult, and to bring childish patterns and reactions into adult organization and regulation.

Developmental transformations lead to discontinuities, and it is recognition of discontinuities which also leads to complex problems in understanding the transference and the patient's life history. What the patient has recalled and constructed has been colored and distorted by personal myth, later experience, and developmental transformation. The problem of discontinuity and the differentiation of genetic and developmental sequences was anticipated by Freud (1920b):

So long as we trace the development from its final outcome backwards, the chain of events appears continuous, and

we feel we have gained in insight which is completely satisfactory or even exhaustive. But if we proceed the reverse
way, if we start from the premises inferred from the analysis and try to follow these up to the final result, then we
no longer get the impression of an inevitable sequence of
events which could not have been otherwise determined.
We notice at once that there might have been another
result, and that we might have been just as well able to
understand and explain the latter. The synthesis is thus
not so satisfactory as the analysis [p. 167].

The problem of reconstructing developmental steps
and sequences, of tracing the overdetermined numerous
factors of pathogenesis, revitalized issues in contemporary
psychoanalysis, both evoke and challenge reconstruction.
The issues of genetic fallacy and adultomorphic myth are
further complicated by the confusion of pathological regression, normal development, and deviant development;
by the number of factors and the varied strength of forces
involved; and by the discontinuities which have to be
bridged. Given the wealth of information provided by the
analytic data, this is not necessarily an impossible task in
an impossible profession. But it is never a simple, veridical,
temporally and dynamically interrelated "red thread" of
connections. The reconstructive inferences depend upon
the totality of analytic data, and not just the transference
alone, on the elaboration and remodeling of the reconstruction in the crucible of the analytic process. Validation
depends upon continuing analysis of the transference and
countertransference in interaction with reconstruction.
The analyst also engages in reciprocal self-examination
and countertransference analysis. The process depends
upon logical and consistent clarification of ambiguities
into the most meaningful and coherent articulation and
fit with the analytic data and the patient's relived and reexamined history.

Therapeutic Value

The analyst's mode of observation, his attending, listening, and selection, his theoretical and personal preferences or prejudices will influence the process of reconstruction. Empathy, introspection, and cognitive deduction, inference, utilization of analytic knowledge and logic are all determinants of reconstruction. Although it can never be entirely free of suggestion or bilateral subjectivity, because of the unique integration of the evidence of the analytic data in reconstruction, it can engender bilateral conviction in patient and analyst that surpasses direct recall. The patient's seemingly assured convictions about his or her life and loved ones so often prove to be unreliable, childish constructions. Here construction and reconstruction are not used interchangeably, but the path from tentative construction to analytic reconstruction involves the controlled and careful use of initial speculation and the gradual and comprehensive unraveling of the patient's analytic and life experience.

Analytic constructions are transformed into reconstructions, which may seem to merge with the analytic process over time. Speculative construction and reasoned reconstruction also alternate with spiraling and often obscure mutual influence. Bilateral curiosity about how the patient came to be that type of person with that type of neurosis is very important to effective reconstruction. No two analysts would necessarily offer identical reconstructions; at best, there may be discrepancies and disjunctions which cannot be synthesized, and mysteries which the analysis cannot solve. Patients reinvent themselves in their myths and historical legends. In analysis, the patient is not "reinvented," or given a new portrait, but his autobiography is revised and recreated in degree, depth, and organization. Psychic change in analysis is facilitated by insightful reconstruction and this therapeutic dimension of reconstruction is prominent in classical clinical analysis.

Beginning analysis with the Rat Man, Freud (1909) offers an early reconstruction to this patient during his first month of treatment. The Rat Man had worked late hours, and between 12 and 1 o'clock at night he would open the door as if his deceased father's ghost were there, and then he would take out and observe his own penis in a mirror. He ambivalently complied with his father's desire for hard work and defied his father by masturbatory play. Freud (1909) recorded the following intervention:

> I ventured to put forward a construction to the effect that when he was a child of under six he had been guilty of some sexual misdemeanour connected with masturbation and had been soundly castigated for it by his father. This punishment, according to my hypothesis, had, it was true, put an end to his masturbating, but on the other hand it had left behind it an ineradicable grudge against his father and had established him for all time in his role of an interferer with the patient's sexual enjoyment. To my great astonishment the patient then informed me that his mother had repeatedly described to him an occurrence of this kind which dated from his earliest childhood and had evidently escaped being forgotten by her on account of its remarkable consequences. He himself, however, had no recollection of it whatever. The tale was as follows. When he was very small—it became possible to establish the date more exactly owing to its having coincided with the fatal illness of an elder sister [p. 235]—he had done something naughty, for which his father had given him a beating [p. 205].

Freud's (1909) process notes slightly varied the timing even earlier and expanded the reconstruction.

> I could not restrain myself here from constructing the material at our disposal into an event: how before the age of six he had been in the habit of masturbating and how his father had forbidden it, using as a threat the phrase "it would be the death of you" and perhaps also threatening to cut off his penis. This would account for his masturbating in connection with the release from the curse, for

the commands and prohibitions in his unconscious and for the threat of death which was now thrown back on to his father. His present suicidal ideas would correspond to a self-reproach of being a murderer [p. 263].

The reconstruction appeared to enlist the Rat Man's interest in reflecting about a genetic explanation of his irrational behavior; free association proceeded with additional relevant memories and with the beginning of an alliance to fill in the blanks and close the gaps in the interrelationship between the patient's childhood experience and his adult disorder. If we assume that in many respects premature reconstruction served defensive intellectualization and resistance to understanding, what was occurring in the analytic situation was nevertheless remarkable. It was a pathfinding analytic effort to help the Rat Man make sense of his life and his neurosis.

The Rat Man's mother confirmed the beating incident, but not as punishment for masturbation. He was beaten by his father because he had bitten someone (biting like a rat), and continued to expect retaliation for his forbidden impulses. The child within was alive, kicking, and biting. The reconstruction itself figured in the subsequent transference reaction, so that conviction came not from memory substitution but from its parallel to and illumination of transference analysis.

In this pioneer period, Freud (1909) referred to "the constant sameness which as a rule characterizes the phantasies that are constructed around the period of childhood, irrespective of how greatly or how little real experiences have contributed towards them" (p. 208). Actually, his own inner dialogue between childhood memories and childhood fantasies continued in his later work and in subsequent psychoanalytic discourse. Fantasy itself was not static, but had its own evolution and developmental transformation. There was always at least a kernel of historical and contemporary truth in the fantasy, "more than one version of the scene (each often differing greatly from the other) may be detected in the patient's unconscious phantasies . . . 'childhood memories' are only consolidated at a later period, usually at the age of puberty; . . . this involves a complicated process of remodelling" (Freud, 1909, p. 206).

This process of the developmental transformation of fantasy was depicted in the different phases of the formation of a beating fantasy. The patients described by Freud (1919) were very seldom beaten in childhood and were not brought up with the help of the rod. The first fantasies certainly appeared before school age, and "anyone who neglects childhood analysis is bound to fall into the most disastrous errors" (p. 183). The first phase of the beating fantasy of a girl involves another child, a boy or a girl, being beaten by the father, most often a hated sibling rival. In the second phase, profound transformations have taken place, and the girl now fantasizes herself being beaten by her father, accompanied by her pleasure. "This second phase is the most important and the most momentous of all. . . . It is never remembered, it has never succeeded in becoming conscious. It is a construction of analysis, but it is no less a necessity on that account" (p. 185). The third phase involves anonymous children instead of one child being beaten; the beater is an adult authority such as a teacher, and the producer of the fantasy is now an onlooker or bystander. This third phase fantasy has an unambiguous, concomitant, conscious, sexual excitement and is a masturbation fantasy. The beating fantasy "may go through the most complicated alterations and elaborations; and punishments and humiliations of another kind may be substituted for the beating itself" (p. 186).

The further developmental transformation of beating fantasies was elaborated by A. Freud (1922).[1] She

---

[1] A historical reconstruction indicates that the analyst–coauthor was also Freud, continuing to reconstruct a developmental path for beating fantasies (Young-Bruehl, 1988).

shows again a three-stage development of the beating fantasy and, as in her first paper, is the precursor of her later concept of developmental lines. The conscious beating fantasies were a regressive, distorted substitute for incestuous father–daughter love between 5 and 6 years of age. By the eighth to tenth years they were replaced by "nice stories," occasionally interrupted by or reverting to the beating fantasies. In the masturbation fantasy, the increasing tension leads to beating, while the "nice" daydreams to forgiveness and reconciliation. The final third stage of fantasy development was to create an independent existence for the private fantasy through externally communicated short stories. This was sublimated masochism. Her knight's sword was beaten into a plowshare by writing, providing a disguised, pleasurable, shared fantasy that was socially accepted and appreciated.

Today, these reconstructions are pioneer paradigms which, despite their timeless intellectual appeal and stimulation, appear rather incomplete and limited. The details of the childhood experiences are lacking, including subtle adversities and traumas. Object relations, especially the mother–child relationship, the parents' relationship to each other, and their attitudes toward the child are hardly represented in comparison with the sexual drive and analsadistic regression. To be sure, the "blow of fate," engendered by the birth of a sibling rival, might be far more serious than physical punishment. The importance of issues of loss, identifications, nonphysical and even nonverbal forms of guilt-inducing and punitive behavior, painful illness, narcissistic injuries, and many other issues, would await later elaboration. An early emphasis on phase-specific, expectable, oedipal trauma was followed by considerations of out-of-phase trauma. Currently, there is an awareness of greater complexity, preoedipal determinants, phase overlap, and the influence of antecedents, selective progression-regression, and phase reorganization which may be beneficial or detrimental.

The history of a masochistic beating fantasy may range from considerations of infantile capacities for soothing and self-soothing, infantile attachment to pain or addiction, to pain-inducing objects or their substitutes all the way through oedipal conflict with guilt over incestuous wishes and adolescent experiences of venereal disease and abortion. Masochistic behavior may attempt to master trauma and prove endurance and survival. The reconstruction of oedipal-phase family romance and/or seductive overstimulation or actual primal scene experience, will be of central importance, as in the sadomasochistic interpretation of the primal scene. But the antecedents and aftermath of the seduction are also significant and are relevant to later masochistic character or perversion, acting out or sublimation of masochistic fantasy. The developmental line may be very difficult if not impossible to construct, but it has been suggested in paranoia (Blum, 1980) and in the longitudinal analytic studies of children (Novick and Novick, 1987).

The evolution of an adolescent beating fantasy could be reconstructed beginning with infantile sadomasochistic struggles. These children's battles with their mothers persist through childhood development, and adult analytic data have benefited from corollary and collaborative evidence from child analysis and infant observation. Pain-seeking results from the internalization of the child's own aggression and the parents' aggression toward the child. The attachment to the painful object and to the painful experience (Valenstein, 1973) and to unhappy experience, predisposes to later oedipal "victimization." Both constitutional and experiential determinants (Weil, 1978) lead to ceaseless struggles within, and with others, beginning before the oedipal phase and continuing thereafter for those with fixed, conscious beating fantasies. Parents of these patients have often exposed the patients to noxious experiences or have failed to protect them from neglect, overstimulation, or abuse.

One patient lost the battle for autonomy and self-directed initiative. He had been regarded as a "holy terror" by his mother when he was a toddler. There was no room for negotiation, and this mother had to win all power struggles. Withdrawal into self-comfort replaced difficult maternal comforting and soothing of the child. The maladaptive pattern continued in his adult fantasy life (Escalona, 1968), and the patient imagined object submission to a cruel, omnipotent, phallic woman. He and his mother had each sought to rule with rage, but he conceded only outwardly. The war raged within, and he had developed refined techniques of passive aggression and defiance. In his adult life he fought against being a "yes man," and championed liberties against encroachment by tyrants. On an oedipal level, the close binding ties represented incest and its prohibition. Though such male patients have been overstimulated, humiliated, and have punished and been punished by their mothers, the father is often the manifest victimizer. This displacement of aggression preserves the primary object and contributes to the later, intense, oedipal rivalry. These preoedipally fixated patients readily regress from oedipal conflict and castration anxiety. Sadomasochistic sexual relationship is then the culmination of a long, complex development which, in the end, includes the adolescent experiences, with the original objects reacting to their children's adolescence. If a parent is intensely jealous of the adolescent or threatened by separation and loss, old quarrels may be renewed and intensified. The sadomasochistic tie which evolved during separation-individuation (Mahler, Pine, and Bergman, 1975) and consolidated in a masochistic Oedipus complex and sadistic superego, will be reactivated and fortified. Contributions from each developmental phase to adult beating fantasy and masochistic character can be established (Maleson, 1984; Blum, 1991). Such analytic work confirms that reconstruction has major theoretical and therapeutic value. The past has shaped and limited the personality and its functioning in the present. Reconstruction facilitates the resolution of the infantile neurosis and restores the continuity and cohesion of the personality synergistic with the psychoanalytic process.

Where the whole family has colluded to "cover up" (e.g., incest or child abuse), reconstruction of the nature and course of the conspiracy of silence will be essential (Shengold, 1989). Confrontations with the analyst's views, the patient's analytic data, and family secrets will emerge with shared efforts to sort out fantasy and reality and ascertain, if possible, "where the truth lies." Even the eyewitness will have his blind spots and subjective bias. The patient will see his parents' confusion or confession in new ways while recognizing his own wishes to not know and to distort and control his own and their responses. There will be partial "truths" and internal changes in the way old, impersonal facts are newly personified and reinterpreted. The process of reconstruction will continue during termination and, in favorable cases, rather silently after the analysis.

In the history of psychoanalysis, reconstruction has replaced memories, which no longer have an exceptional position in clinical psychoanalysis. A previously repressed memory or factual experience may have a special significance at a particular point in analysis, to be determined in terms of unconscious transference conflict and fantasy, and as a genetic determinant in terms of reconstruction. Some analysts use reconstruction as a specialized technique, others as a regular dimension of interpretation, and many as an explanatory framework that guides interpretation. It is important that the locus of inference and intervention should freely oscillate between present and past coordinates. Reconstruction seeks to synthesize scattered and fragmented analytic data; it is a rational, analytic explanation and exposition of infantile neurotic phenomena and of what has remained childish in the patient. Therapeutically, reconstruction aims at reclaiming lost childhood and the child living in the adult, in order for mature reintegration to take place. The genetic antecedents are the paths taken to the patient's present position and the prototypes of irrational repetition.

The therapeutic value of reconstruction cannot be artificially separated from its validity or its "truth value." Involved here is not just hermeneutic meaning or narrative fit, but cause, consequence, and genetic–developmental, temporal sequence. The patient and the analyst come to understand how the patient idiosyncratically misinterprets, often in a characteristic style (Reed, 1991) and something of how and why; for example, certain defensive maneuvers and identifications with the aggressor and victim may be used.

Reconstruction may be of some value in the understanding of the origin of more recently recognized impairments in addition to traditional analytic work in the area of psychic conflict. Structural deficits and developmental arrests, deviations, and disharmonies are now commonly detected in many seriously ill patients, interwoven with intrapsychic conflict. Such deficits and deviations may be a consequence of conflict or an influence in the evolution and resolution of conflict. How helpful genetic interpretation and reconstruction may be for such problems is a research issue, but reconstruction has been crucial in the reversal of transference psychosis (Wallerstein, 1967). On the other hand, reconstruction for such severely psychotic patients as Schreber (Freud, 1911) would probably have little or no therapeutic effect, but it might have important theoretical value. This is apparent in contemporary reconstructions of the Schreber case (Niederland, 1974). Reconstruction could help elucidate a patient's psychotic adaptation and also the development of his profound psychopathology. The "grain of historic truth in a delusion" is a reconstruction that has had very valuable theoretical and technical implications.

An inexact, relatively inaccurate reconstruction could be psychotherapeutically useful, but not really analytically beneficial. A wrong interpretation or reconstruction does not advance the psychoanalytic process. A reconstruction could also be correct without being appropriate or beneficial; it could be correct without being related to what the reconstruction purports to explain; it could be partially accurate and subject to correction and reformulation (Strenger, 1991). Actually, there is always a bilateral evaluation of the accuracy of reconstruction, with more or less conviction or doubt.

In the pioneer period of psychoanalysis, analysts found exciting support for their clinical reconstructions in reports of the patient's family and family friends or in old documents and records. Analytic patients may be stimulated to seek and, indeed, find such direct external confirmation of analytic reconstructions. Marie Bonaparte (1945) confirmed Freud's reconstruction of her early childhood primal scene experience. Upon questioning, her servant disclosed having had such sexual relations in her presence. This type of extraclinical confirmation may be welcome, but it is unnecessary. The reports of relatives or servants may or may not be reliable. Further confirmation may be obtained in simultaneous or subsequent analysis of parent and child (Levy, 1960; Barglow, Jaffe, and Vaughn, 1989), but it is the confluence of all the evidence gathered in the course of the analysis that fortifies conviction. The enormous mass of data in clinical analysis provides ample material for the process of reconstruction.

Many reconstructions are repeatedly confirmed in their core configuration even as they are elaborated and amended in later analytic work. The compelling convergence of data from different modes of observation and from different sources validates reconstruction and advances analytic research.

The evidence of the reconstruction and its derivation from and role in the analytic process codetermine the limits of both the clinical value and the analytic validity of the reconstruction. No two analysts will have identical reconstructions, but within the same theoretical framework, the reconstructions may be expected to be overlapping and complementary or supplementary. From practice to theory and from theory to practice, reconstruction is an integral and integrative dimension of psychoanalysis. It is impossible to envision an analytic process without implicit and explicit reconstruction, and reconstruction is an essential dimension of psychoanalysis.

References

Abrams, S. (1984), Fantasy and reality in the oedipal phase. *The Psychoanalytic Study of the Child*, 39:83–100. New Haven, CT: Yale University Press.

Anthi, R. (1983), Reconstruction of preverbal experiences. *J. Amer. Psychoanal. Assn.*, 31:3–32.

Arlow, J. A. (1987), The dynamics of interpretation. *Psychoanal. Quart.*, 56:68–87.

———— (1991), Methodology and reconstruction. *Psychoanal. Quart.*, 60:539–563.

Barglow, P., Jaffe, C., & Vaughn, B. (1989), Psychoanalytic reconstructions and empirical data. *J. Amer. Psychoanal. Assn.*, 37:401–436.

Bergen, M. E. (1958), The effect of severe trauma on a four-year-old child. *The Psychoanalytic Study of the Child*, 13:407–429. New York: International Universities Press.

Bergman, P., & Escalona, S. (1949), Unusual sensitivities in very young children. *The Psychoanalytic Study of the Child*, 3/4:333–352. New York: International Universities Press.

Bergmann, M., & Jucovy, M., eds. (1982), *Generations of the Holocaust*. New York: Basic Books.

Berliner, B. (1947), On some psychodynamics of masochism. *Psychoanal. Quart.*, 16:459–471.

Blum, H. P. (1974), The borderline childhood of the Wolf Man. *J. Amer. Psychoanal. Assn.*, 22:721–742.

———— (1977), The prototype of preoedipal reconstruction. *J. Amer. Psychoanal. Assn.*, 25:757–785.

———— (1978), Reconstruction in a case of postpartum depression. *The Psychoanalytic Study of the Child*, 33:335–362. New Haven, CT: Yale University Press.

References

———— (1979), On the concept and consequences of the primal scene. *Psychoanal. Quart.*, 48:27–47.

———— (1980), The value of reconstruction in adult psychoanalysis. *Internat. J. Psycho-Anal.*, 61:39–54.

———— (1981), Some current and recurrent problems of psychoanalytic technique. *J. Amer. Psychoanal. Assn.*, 29:47–68.

———— (1983), The position and value of extratransference interpretation. *J. Amer. Psychoanal. Assn.*, 31:587–618.

———— (1986), The concept of reconstruction of trauma. In: *The Reconstruction of Trauma*, ed. A. Rothstein. Madison, CT: International Universities Press, pp. 7–27.

———— (1987), The role of identification in the resolution of trauma: The Anna Freud Memorial Lecture. *Psychoanal. Quart.*, 56:609–627.

———— (1989), Punitive parenthood and childhood trauma. In: *The Psychoanalytic Core: Essays in Honor of Leo Rangell*. Madison, CT: International Universities Press, pp. 167–186.

———— (1991), Affect theory and the theory of technique. *J. Amer. Psychoanal. Assn.*, 39 (suppl.):265–290.

Bonaparte, M. (1945), Notes on the analytical discovery of a primal scene. *The Psychoanalytic Study of the Child*, 1:119–126. New York: International Universities Press.

Brenman, E. (1980), The value of reconstruction in adult psychoanalysis. *Internat. J. Psycho-Anal.*, 61:53–60.

Brenner, C. (1968), Psychoanalysis and science. *J. Amer. Psychoanal. Assn.*, 16:675–696.

Breuer, J., & Freud, S. (1895), Studies on Hysteria. *Standard Edition*, 2. London: Hogarth Press, 1955.

Cohen, D. J. (1980), Constructive and reconstructive activities in the analysis of a depressed child. *The Psychoanalytic Study of the Child*, 35:237–266. New Haven, CT: Yale University Press.

Cohler, B. (1981), Adult developmental psychology and reconstruction in psychoanalysis. In: *The Course of Life*, Vol. 3, ed. S. Greenspan & G. Pollock. Washington, DC: U.S. Department of Heath & Human Services, pp. 149–199.

Coltrera, J. T. (1979), Truth from genetic illusion: The transference and the fate of the infantile neurosis. *J. Amer. Psychoanal. Assn.*, 27 (suppl.):289–313.

Davidoff-Hirsch, H. (1985), Oedipal and preoedipal phenomena. *J. Amer. Psychoanal. Assn.*, 33:821–840.

Ekstein, R., & Rangell, L. (1961), Reconstruction and theory formation. *J. Amer. Psychoanal. Assn.*, 9:684–697.

Escalona, S. A. (1968), *The Roots of Individuality*. Chicago: Aldine Press.

Esman, A. H. (1973), The primal scene. *The Psychoanalytic Study of the Child*, 28:49–81. New Haven, CT: Yale University Press.

References

—— (1983), The stimulus barrier. *The Psychoanalytic Study of the Child*, 38:193–208. New Haven, CT: Yale University Press.

Etchegoyen, H. (1982), The relevance of here and now transference interpretation for the reconstruction of early psychic development. *Internat. J. Psycho-Anal.*, 63:65–75.

Faimberg, H., & Corel, A. (1990), Repetition and surprise. *Internat. J. Psycho-Anal.*, 71:411–420.

Fenichel, O. (1945), *The Psychoanalytic Theory of Neurosis*. New York: W. W. Norton.

Frank, A. (1969), The unrememberable and the unforgettable. *The Psychoanalytic Study of the Child*, 24:48–77. New York: International Universities Press.

—— (1990), Psychic change and the analyst as biographer. *Internat. J. Psycho-Anal.*, 72:22–26.

Freud, A. (1922), Beating fantasies and daydreams. *The Writings*, 1:137–157. New York: International Universities Press, 1974.

—— (1951), Observations on child development. *The Writings*, 4:143–162. New York: International Universities Press.

—— (1967), Comments on trauma. In: *Psychic Trauma*, ed. S. S. Furst. New York: Basic Books, pp. 235–245.

—— (1969), Difficulties in the path of psychoanalysis. *The Writings*, 7:124–156. New York: International Universities Press.

—— (1970), The infantile neurosis. *The Writings*, 7:189–203. New York: International Universities Press.

—— Burlingham, D. (1944), Infants without families. *The Writings*, 3:543–634. New York: International Universities Press.

Freud, S. (1892–1899), Extracts from the Fliess papers. *Standard Edition*, 1:173–397. London: Hogarth Press, 1950.

—— (1896a), Further remarks on the neuro-psychoses of defence. *Standard Edition*, 3:159–185. London: Hogarth Press, 1962.

—— (1896b), Heredity and the aetiology of the neuroses. *Standard Edition*, 3:141–156. London: Hogarth Press, 1962.

—— (1896c), Sexuality in the aetiology of the neuroses. *Standard Edition*, 3:259–285. London: Hogarth Press, 1962.

—— (1899), Screen memories. *Standard Edition*, 3:301–322. London: Hogarth Press, 1962.

—— (1905), Fragments of an analysis of a case of hysteria. *Standard Edition*, 7:3–122. London: Hogarth Press, 1953.

—— (1909), Notes upon a case of obsessional neurosis. *Standard Edition*, 10:153–320. London: Hogarth Press, 1955.

—— (1911), Psycho-analytic notes on an autobiographical account of a case of paranoia. *Standard Edition*, 12:3–82. London: Hogarth Press, 1958.

—— (1912), The dynamics of transference. *Standard Edition*, 12:97–108. London: Hogarth Press, 1958.

References

—————— (1913), Totem and Taboo. *Standard Edition*, 13:1–162. London: Hogarth Press, 1955.

—————— (1914a), On the history of the psycho-analytic movement. *Standard Edition*, 14:4–66. London: Hogarth Press, 1957.

—————— (1914b), Remembering, repeating and working-through. *Standard Edition*, 12:145–156. London: Hogarth Press, 1958.

—————— (1914c), On narcissism. *Standard Edition*, 14:67–102. London: Hogarth Press, 1957.

—————— (1916–1917), Introductory Lectures on Psycho-Analysis. *Standard Edition*, 15 & 16. London: Hogarth Press, 1963.

—————— (1918), From the history of an infantile neurosis. *Standard Edition*, 17:3–123. London: Hogarth Press, 1955.

—————— (1919), 'A child is being beaten.' *Standard Edition*, 17:175–204. London: Hogarth Press, 1955.

—————— (1920a), Beyond the Pleasure Principle. *Standard Edition*, 18:3–64. London: Hogarth Press, 1955.

—————— (1920b), The psychogenesis of a case of homosexuality in a woman. *Standard Edition*, 18:145–172. London: Hogarth Press, 1955.

—————— (1923), The Ego and the Id. *Standard Edition*, 19:3–66. London: Hogarth Press, 1961.

—————— (1926a), Inhibitions, symptoms and anxiety. *Standard Edition*, 20:77–175. London: Hogarth Press, 1959.

—————— (1926b), The question of lay analysis. *Standard Edition*, 20:179–258. London: Hogarth Press, 1959.

—————— (1930), Civilization and its discontents. *Standard Edition*, 21:59–145. London: Hogarth Press, 1961.

—————— (1933), New Introductory Lectures on Psycho-Analysis. *Standard Edition*, 22:3–182. London: Hogarth Press, 1964.

—————— (1937), Constructions in analysis. *Standard Edition*, 23:255–269. London: Hogarth Press, 1964.

—————— (1939), Moses and Monotheism. *Standard Edition*, 23:3–137. London: Hogarth Press, 1964.

—————— (1940), An outline of psycho-analysis. *Standard Edition*, 23:141–207. London: Hogarth Press, 1964.

Friedman, L. (1983), Reconstruction and the like. *Psychoanal. Inquiry*, 3:189–222.

Furst, S. S., ed. (1967), *Psychic Trauma*. New York: Basic Books.

—————— (1986), Psychic trauma and its reconstruction with particular reference to postchildhood trauma. In: *The Reconstruction of Trauma*, ed. A. Rothstein. New York: International Universities Press, pp. 29–39.

Gill, M. (1982), *The Analysis of Transference*. Vol. 1. New York: International Universities Press.

Glenn, J. (1984), Psychic trauma and masochism. *J. Amer. Psychoanal. Assn.*, 32:357–380.

References

Glover, E. (1955), *The Technique of Psychoanalysis*. New York: International Universities Press.

Greenacre, P. (1956), Re-evaluation of the process of working-through. *Internat. J. Psycho-Anal.*, 37:439–444.

—— (1967), The influence of infantile trauma on genetic patterns. In: *Psychic Trauma*, ed. S. S. Furst. New York: Basic Books, pp. 108–153.

—— (1975), On reconstruction. *J. Amer. Psychoanal. Assn.*, 23:693–771.

—— (1979), Reconstruction and the process of individuation. *The Psychoanalytic Study of the Child*, 34:121–144. New Haven, CT: Yale University Press.

—— (1980), A historical sketch of the use and disuse of reconstruction. *The Psychoanalytic Study of the Child*, 35:35–40. New Haven, CT: Yale University Press.

—— (1981), Reconstruction: Its nature and therapeutic value. *J. Amer. Psychoanal. Assn.*, 29:27–46.

Hartmann, H. (1939), *Ego Psychology and the Problem of Adaptation*. New York: International Universities Press, 1958.

Isakower, O. (1938), A contribution to the pathopsychology of phenomena associated with falling asleep. *Internat. J. Psycho-Anal.*, 19:331–345.

Jacobs, T. (1991), The relationships between transferences and reconstruction. In: *The Uses of the Self*. Madison, CT: International Universities Press, pp. 75–100.

Jacobson, E. (1964), *The Self and the Object World*. New York: International Universities Press.

Kanzer, M. (1953), Past and present in the transference. *J. Amer. Psychoanal. Assn.*, 1:144–154.

Kardina, A. (1977), *My Analysis with Freud*. New York. W. W. Norton.

Kennedy, H. (1971), Problems in reconstruction in child analysis. *The Psychoanalytic Study of the Child*, 26:386–402. Chicago: Quadrangle.

Kernberg, O. F. (1975), *Borderline Conditions and Pathological Narcissism*. New York: Jason Aronson.

Kestenberg, J. (1972), How children remember and parents forget. *Internat. J. Psychoanal. Psychother.*, 1/2:103–123.

Khan, M. (1963), The concept of cumulative trauma. *The Psychoanalytic Study of the Child*, 18:286–306. New York: International Universities Press.

Knight, R. P. (1953), Borderline states. In: *Drives, Affects, Behavior*, ed. R. M. Loewenstein. New York: International Universities Press, pp. 203–215.

Kohut, H. (1971), *The Analysis of the Self*. New York: International Universities Press.

References

Kramer, S. (1983), Object-coercive doubting. In: *Defense and Resistance*, ed. H. P. Blum. New York: International Universities Press, pp. 325–352.

——— (1990), Residues of incest. In: *Adult Analysis and Childhood Sexual Abuse*, ed. H. Levine. Hillsdale, NJ: Analytic Press, pp. 149–170.

Kris, E. (1956a), On some vicissitudes of insight in psychoanalysis. *Internat. J. Psycho-Anal.*, 37:445–455.

——— (1956b), The personal myth. *J. Amer. Psychoanal. Assn.*, 4:653–681.

——— (1956c), The recovery of childhood memories in psychoanalysis. *The Psychoanalytic Study of the Child*, 11:54–88. New York: International Universities Press.

Kris Study Group (1971), Recollection and Reconstruction in Psychoanalysis, *Kris Study Group*, Monograph 4, ed. B. Fine, E. Joseph, & H. Waldhorn. New York: International Universities Press.

Levine, H., ed. (1990), *Adult Analysis and Childhood Sexual Abuse*. Hillsdale, NJ: Analytic Press.

Levy, K. (1960), Simultaneous analysis of a mother and her adolescent daughter. *The Psychoanalytic Study of the Child*, 15:378–394. New York: International Universities Press.

Lewin, B. D. (1955), Dream psychology and the analytic situation. *Psychoanal. Quart.*, 24:169–199.

Loewenstein, R. M. (1951), The problem of interpretation. *Psychoanal. Quart.*, 20:1–14.

Mahler, M. S. (1971), A study of the separation–individuation process and its possible application to borderline phenomena in the psychoanalytic situation. *The Psychoanalytic Study of the Child*, 26:403–424. New York: Quadrangle.

——— McDevitt, J. B. (1980), The separation-individuation process and identity formation. In: *The Course of Life*, Vol. 1, ed. S. I. Greenspan & G. H. Pollock. Washington, DC: U.S. Department of Health & Human Services, pp. 395–406.

——— Pine, F., & Bergman, A. (1975), *The Psychological Birth of the Human Infant*. New York: Basic Books.

Maleson, F. (1984), The multiple meanings of masochism in psychoanalytic discourse. *J. Amer. Psychoanal. Assn.*, 32:325–356.

Masson, J., ed. (1985), *The Complete Letters of Sigmund Freud to Wilhelm Fliess*, 1887–1904. Cambridge: Harvard University Press.

Neubauer, P. B. (1967), Trauma and psychopathology. In: *Psychic Trauma*, ed. S. S. Furst. New York: Basic Books, pp. 85–107.

——— (1979), The role of insight in psychoanalysis. *J. Amer. Psychoanal. Assn.*, 27 (suppl.):29–40.

Niederland, W. G. (1968), Clinical observations on the survivor syndrome. *Internat. J. Psycho-Anal.*, 49:313–315.

References

——— (1974), *The Schreber Case*. New York: Quadrangle.

Novey, S. (1968), *The Second Look*. Baltimore, MD: Johns Hopkins University Press.

Novick, K., & Novick, J. (1987), The essence of masochism. *The Psychoanalytic Study of the Child*, 42:353–384. New Haven, CT: Yale University Press.

Panel (1982), Construction and reconstruction. A Malin, reporter. *J. Amer. Psychoanal. Assn.*, 30:213–233.

Pollock, G. (1970), Anniversary reactions, trauma, and mourning. *Psychoanal. Quart.*, 39:347–371.

Rangell, L. (1967), The metapsychology of psychic trauma. In: *Psychic Trauma*, ed. S. S. Furst. New York: Basic Books, pp. 51–84.

——— (1989), The significance of infant observations for psychoanalysis in later stages of life. In: *The Significance of Infant Observational Research for Clinical Work with Children, Adolescents, and Adults*, ed. S. Dowling & A. Rothstein. New York: International Universities Press, pp. 195–211.

Rank, O. (1924), *The Trauma of Birth*. New York: Harcourt Brace, 1929.

Reed, G. (1991), On the value of explicit reconstruction. *Psychoanal. Quart.*, (in press).

Rees, K. (1978), The child's understanding of his past. *The Psychoanalytic Study of the Child*, 33:237–259. New Haven, CT: Yale University Press.

Reider, N. (1953), Reconstruction and screen formation. *J. Amer. Psychoanal. Assn.*, 1:389–405.

Rosen, V. H. (1953), The reconstruction of a traumatic childhood event in a case of derealization. *J. Amer. Psychoanal. Assn.*, 3:211–221.

Sachs, O. (1967), Distinctions between fantasy and reality elements in memory and reconstruction. *Internat. J. Psycho-Anal.*, 48:416–423.

Sandler, J., & Sandler, A.-M. (1983), The "second censorship," and some technical implications. *Internat. J. Psycho-Anal.*, 64:413–425.

Schafer, R. (1980), *Narrative Action in Psychoanalysis*. Worcester, Mass.: Clark University Press.

——— (1983), *The Analytic Attitude*. New York: Basic Books.

Schimek, J. (1975), The interpretations of the past. *J. Amer. Psychoanal. Assn.*, 23:845–865.

——— (1977), Fact and fantasy in the seduction theory. *J. Amer. Psychoanal. Assn.*, 35:937–966.

Shapiro, T., & Stern, D. (1989), Psychoanalytic perspectives on the first year of life. In: *The Course of Life*, Vol. 1, ed. S. I. Greenspan & G. H. Pollock. Madison, CT: International Universities Press, pp. 271–292.

References

Shengold, L. (1989), *Soul Murder*. New Haven, CT: Yale University Press.

Silverman, M. (1989), Infant observation and the reconstruction of early experience. In: *The Significance of Infant Observational Research for Clinical Work with Children, Adolescents, and Adults*, ed. S. Dowling & A. Rothstein. Madison, CT: International Universities Press.

Solnit, A. J. (1982), Early psychic development as reflected in the psychoanalytic process. *Internat. J. Psycho-Anal.*, 63:23–37.

Spence, D. (1982), *Narrative Truth and Historical Truth*. New York: W. W. Norton.

———— (1987), *The Freudian Metaphor*. New York: W. W. Norton.

Spitz, R. A. (1965), *The First Year of Life*. New York: International Universities Press.

Strenger, C. (1991), *Between Hermeneutics and Science*. Madison, CT: International Universities Press.

Valenstein, A. (1973), On attachment to painful feelings and the negative therapeutic reaction. *The Psychoanalytic Study of the Child*, 28:305–392. New Haven, CT: Yale University Press.

———— (1989), Pre-oedipal reconstructions in psychoanalysis. *Internat. J. Psycho-Anal.*, 70:433–442.

Wallerstein, R. (1967), Reconstruction and mastery in the transference psychosis. *J. Amer. Psychoanal. Assn.*, 15:551–583.

Weil, A. (1970), The basic core. *The Psychoanalytic Study of the Child*, 25:442–460. New York: International Universities Press.

———— (1978), Maturational variations and genetic-dynamic issues. *J. Amer. Psychoanal. Assn.*, 26:461–491.

Wetzler, S. (1985), The historical truth of psychoanalytic reconstructions. *Internat. Rev. Psychoanal.*, 12:187–197.

Williams, M. (1987), Reconstruction of an early seduction and its aftereffects. *J. Amer. Psychoanal. Assn.*, 35:145–163.

Winnicott, D. W. (1965), *The Maturational Processes and the Facilitating Environment*. London: Hogarth Press.

Young-Bruehl, E. (1988), *Anna Freud*. New York: Summit Books.

Name Index

187

Name Index

Kanzer, M., 159
Kennedy, H., 111, 121
Kernberg, O. F., 24
Kestenberg, J., 150
Khan, M., 47, 55, 135
Klein, M., 24
Knight, R. P., 24
Kohut, H., 24
Kramer, S., vii, 51, 104
Kris, E., 1, 10, 25–26, 29, 63–64, 84, 93–
    94, 115, 122, 128, 134, 135, 159,
    163
Kris, M., vii

Levine, H., 104–105
Levy, K., 176
Lewin, B. D., 26
Loewenstein, R. M., 86

Mahler, M. S., 24, 31, 43, 110, 173
Maleson, F., 174
Masson, J., 139
McDevitt, J. B., vii, 43

Neubauer, P. B., vii, 49, 122, 135
Niederland, W. G., 65, 176
Novey, S., 22, 147, 165
Novick, J., 172
Novick, K., 172
Nunberg, H., vii

Orwell, G., 60
Ostow, M., vii

Pacella, B., vii
Pine, F., 31, 110, 173
Pollock, G., 48

Rangell, L., 19, 49, 56, 149
Rank, O., 44
Reed, G., 175
Reider, N., 26, 128, 160–161
Rosen, V. H., 26, 101
Rothstein, A., 41n

Sachs, O., 149
Schafer, R., 134, 140, 142
Schimek, J., 130, 138
Shapiro, T., 43
Shengold, L., vii, 103, 106, 174
Spence, D., 25, 52, 134, 141, 142–143,
    144, 164–165
Spitz, R. A., 31
Stern, D., 43
Strachey, 43–44
Strenger, C., 176

Valenstein, A., vii, 172
Vaughn, B., 176

Waldhorn, H., 26, 135, 164
Wallerstein, R., 175
Weil, A., vii, viii, 138, 172
Wetzler, S., 134, 149
Winnicott, D. W., 31
Wordsworth, W., 17

Young-Bruehl, E., 170n

Subject Index

Subject Index

Childhood
actual experience of, 26–27
in clinical psychoanalysis, 127–128
conflicts of, 17–18, 32, 85–86, 133
–134. *See also* Unconscious
conflicts
developmental significance of, 1
inner life and fantasies of, 9
reconstruction of, 141–142
recreation of, 157
traumas and patterns of, 16
unresolved conflicts of, 128
Childhood seduction, 24–25. *See also* Seduction theory
contemporary reconstruction and,
89–108
fantasy of, 27, 29, 32–33
libidinal factors in, 45
"memories" of, 42
silent complicity in, 50–51, 97–100
Circumcision, reconstruction of effects
of, 70–87
Civilization and Its Discontents, 129
Clarification, 156–157
Cognitive deduction, 167
Cognitive development stages, 2
Coherence, 143–144
Collusive secrets, 155
Condensation, 164–165
Conflicts. *See also* Childhood, conflicts
of; Unconscious conflicts
identification of, 135
unresolved, 128
Conspiracy of silence, 50–51, 97–100,
174
Constitutional factors, 30
Constructions, 5–6, 20
analytic, 10, 167
as analytic hypotheses, 7, 21
as cocomposition, 153
versus reconstruction, 46–47
Constructs, preliminary, 112–113
Continuity, 11
genetic, 110–111
search for, 1

Countertransference, 133–134
analysis of, 166
in childhood seduction, 107–108
Cross-dressing, 81

Death
fear of, 164
of parent, 62
trauma of, 48–49
Defense analysis, 29–30
Defensive constellations, 153
Delinquent destructiveness, 59–60
Denial
of physical illness, 79–80
of traumatic event, 48–51, 61–62
Depressive reactions, 106
Developmental arrests, understanding
of, 175–176
Developmental knowledge, 1–2
Developmental phases
overlap of, 83
in reconstruction, 78–87
Developmental propositions, 7
Developmental research, ix
Developmental strain, 96–97
Developmental transformation, 138–
139, 165–166
of fantasy, 170–171
Discrete events, 9–10
Displacement, 164–165
Dogmatism, 143
Dora case, 32–33
cumulative trauma in, 89
denial of seduction in, 50
Dreams, 23
childhood memories and, 91–92
in reconstruction process, 39, 101–
102
Drive development, 31

Ego
differentiation of and psychic trauma,
66–67
endowment, 30
fragility of, 54–55

Subject Index

Invulnerables, 58

Language
  receptive and expressive, 122–123
  structure of, 2
Libido theory, 30, 31, 43
Living conditions, trauma and, 67–68

Magical identifications, 81–82
Masochistic fantasies, transformation of,
    170–174
Masturbation
  conflict and guilt in, 96
  fantasy and, 114
  fear of aggression and, 117–118
  primal scene fantasy and, 118–119
  punishment for, 105
Meaning, 162
Memory. *See also* Screen memories
  accuracy of, 13
  assumptions about, 138
  fragmentary, 28
  gaps in, 18–19, 20, 46–47
  incomplete, 127
  as living record of past, 18
  phylogenetic, 130
  psychic reality of, 83
  versus reconstruction, 10–11, 22
  resistance to, 164–165
  shaping of, 140–141
  suppression of, 100–101
  telescoping of, 139
Moses and Monotheism, 129
Mother
  denial of illness of, 76–77, 79–80
  hostility toward, 103–104
  intrapsychic experience of during
      pregnancy and birth, 114
Mother-child relationship, fantasy ver-
      sus actual, 116
Myth
  adultomorphic, 166
  personal, 1, 29, 145

Nature-nurture duality, 30

Neurosis
  genesis of, 151–152
  reconstruction in analysis of, 69–87
  role of past in, 17–18
  traumatic, 52–54
Night terrors, 63
Nightmares, 63

Obesity, devouring fantasies and, 36
Object loss, 72
  trauma and, 44
Object relations, 31
  theory of, 2
Observation bias, 139–140
Observation modes, 167
Oedipal issues, 2
Oedipal transference, 103–104
Oedipus complex, 42
Overstimulation, 43, 44–45, 67
  pathogenic influence of, 68

Parapraxis, 19–20, 22
Parents
  abusive, 60–61
  death of, 62
  psychotic, 142
  as seducers, 45, 96–97
Past
  analytic myth of, 13
  analytically determined, 36–37
  causal connections of with present, 11
  continued reinterpretation of, 131–
      132
  creation of, 4–5
  illumination of, 33–35
  importance of, 17–18
  in reconstruction, 35–37
Past-present integration, 11, 21
Pathogenesis theories, 24
  seduction, 29
Patterning, 10
Personal myth, 1
  versus actual experience, 145
  analytic interest in, 29
Personality

Subject Index

childish areas of, 128
cohesion of, 146–147
past in shaping, 17–18, 20–21
regression of, onset of, 155–156
trauma and, 41–42, 56–57
vulnerability to trauma and, 65–66
Phallic preoccupation, 73–77, 80–81
Phase-related disturbance, 10
Phobia, origins of, 19
Physical illness
denial of, 79–80
neurosis and, 69–87
Pluralism, 143
Preoedipal affective attunement, 36
Preoedipal problems, 2
Primal scene
cultural condoning of, 67–68
fantasy and experience of, 118–119
meaning of, 138–139
reconstruction of, 176
role of, 114
sadomasochistic interpretation of, 76, 172
trauma of, 45–46
traumatic consequences of, 129–130
Protective shield concept, 43
Psychic determinism, 143–144
Psychic mechanisms, 139
Psychic reality
external reality and, 147–148
in reconstruction, 158
reconstruction and, 127–150
Psychic trauma, 66–67
Psychoanalysis
early aim of, 19–20
meaning in, 138–140
narrative aspect of, 140–141
pioneer period of, 176–177
reconstruction concept in, 17–39
reconstruction in, 1–16
science of, 51–52
therapeutic value of reconstruction in, 151–177
trauma reconstruction in, 41–68
Psychological trauma, 61

Psychosomatic reactions, 57
Punishment fantasies, 129–130

Rage, trauma-related, 64
Rapists, childhood trauma of, 59–60
Rat Man case
punishment fantasies in, 129–130
reconstruction in, 168–169
Reality. See also External reality; Psychic reality
versus fantasy, 129–130
internal and external, 147–148
unknowability of, 145
Rearrangement, 139
Reciprocal illumination, 156
Reconstruction
of actual past, 35–37
in analysis of five-year-old, 109–126
in analysis of neurotic and physical illness, 69–87
in analytic process, 21–23
approximate, 122
childhood seduction and, 89–108
contemporary, 158
decline in interest in, 130–131
definition of, 5
developmental theory and, 2
discreteness of, 12–13
dream analysis in, 39
ego psychological approach to, 134–135
facilitating effects and thrust of, 161
factors in, 153–154
Freudian model of, 5–6
genetic-developmental views in, 4
genetic interpretation and, 22
identification and developmental phase considerations in, 78–87
incorrect, 128
influences on, ix
versus interpretation, 10–12
limits of, 149
of missing memory, 46–47
principles of, 37–38

Subject Index

Subject Index